LIVING OFF THE GRID

Other Books by Gary Collins

Going Off The Grid: The How-To Book of
Simple Living and Happiness

The Simple Life Guide To RV Living: The Road to Freedom
and The Mobile Lifestyle Revolution

The Simple Life Guide To Optimal Health: How to
Get Healthy, Lose Weight, Reverse Disease and
Feel Better Than Ever

LIVING OFF THE GRID

WHAT TO EXPECT WHILE LIVING THE LIFE OF ULTIMATE FREEDOM AND TRANQUILITY

GARY COLLINS, MS

Living Off The Grid: What to Expect While Living the Life of Ultimate Freedom and Tranquility

First Edition

Printed in the United States of America

Copyright ©2019

Published by Second Nature Publishing, Albuquerque, NM 87109

For information about special discounts for bulk purchasing, and/or direct inquiries about copyright, permission, reproduction and publishing inquiries, send request to: contact@secondnaturepublishing.com.

Cover and interior design by Laurie Griffin | www.LaurieGriffin.com

DISCLAIMER OF WARRANTY

The intent of this material is to further educate you in the area of living off the grid.

The text and other related materials are for informational purposes only. The data, author's opinions, and information contained herein are based upon information from various published and unpublished sources that represent the mobile living lifestyle and practice summarized by the author and publisher. Even though the author has been as thorough as possible in his research, the publisher of this text makes no warranties, expressed or implied, regarding the currency, completeness, or scientific accuracy of this information, nor does it warrant the fitness of the information for any particular purpose. Any claims or presentations regarding any specific products or brand names are strictly the responsibility of the product owners or manufacturers. This summary of information from unpublished sources, books, research journals, articles, and the author's opinions are not intended to replace the advice or recommendations by professionals.

Due to the great variability of people living off the grid, and so forth, the author and Second Nature Publishing assume no responsibility for personal injury, property damage, or loss from actions inspired by information in this book. Always consult professionals first. When in doubt, ask for advice. Recommendations in this book are no substitute for the directives of professionals, manufacturers, or federal, state, and local regulatory officials.

ISBN 978-1-57067-373-3

FSC
www.fsc.org
MIX
Paper from
responsible sources
FSC® C005010

Get Your Free Goodies and Be a Part of My Special Community!

Building a solid relationship with my readers is very important to me and is one of the rewards of being a writer. From time to time, I send out my newsletter (never spammy, I promise) to keep you up-to-date with special offers and information about anything new I may be doing. I've moved away from using social media in the pursuit of a simpler life, so if you want to be part of the "in crowd," my newsletter and blog are the place to be.

If that's not enough enticement, when you sign up for my newsletter I'll send you some spectacular free stuff! ☺

- The complete list of my solar system products and components

- My list of essential living-off-the-grid products and resources

You can get all the goodies above by signing up for my mailing list at http://thesimplelifenow.com/offgridliving.

TABLE OF CONTENTS

INTRODUCTION

What Is This Book About?

My first book, *Going Off The Grid,* outlined the beginning of my off-grid adventure, mostly discussing how I found my property, the steps involved in putting together the infrastructure, and the eventual building of my house. This adventure started several years ago (heck, it's hard to believe my original plan of living a more remote lifestyle started over ten years ago as I write this today!), and it just made sense to write a follow-up book discussing what I've learned while living off the grid.

As I've said in the past, everyone who pursues an off-grid life does it a little bit differently. There's no master template that everyone follows. There are so many factors that go into this type of life that there's no way to simply copy, step-by-step, what someone else has done. That doesn't mean you can't learn from others living this lifestyle, though, as most of us take pieces of what others have done and combine it with a lot of trial and error. And trust me, there's a lot of trial and error.

It's also important for me to define what living off the grid means to me, as there are many different definitions floating around out there today. For me, it's simply living on a piece of land that's not attached to any public utilities. Now that doesn't mean you'll have to forego having a working toilet, internet access, TV, or reliable power. Technology has come a long way since the hippies of the 1960s, who I consider to be the pioneers when talking about living the off-grid life. Today you can live remotely, not tied to public utilities, and have a very comfortable lifestyle with most of the creature comforts found in the typical residential tract home. As some of you know, I've been running a successful business remotely for several years now, which includes shipping products, running a website, being interviewed for podcasts, radio and TV, and, of course, writing and publishing books.

That's not to say that all of the above is easy; far from it. It takes a lot of work, but I wouldn't trade it for anything. The point I want to drive home is anyone can do it. This is not just a lifestyle for single people, the rich, or people with mobile businesses—I've met so many diverse people with completely different lives that I know for a fact, if you want it you can have it too!

For those looking to explore living off the grid or a more remote lifestyle, I'll share with you the things I've learned during my adventure. As always, I don't just share the good stuff, but my missteps and mistakes made along the way too. As nothing is learned when things come easy, the lessons are in the true struggles in life and how you react to them. Trust me, there were many times when I wanted to throw in the towel, but something inside me knew the reward at the end was just too good to give up.

With that being said, even if you're already living off the grid, I think you'll learn something new in this book that could possibly make your adventure a little more enjoyable, or give you an idea to make your life a bit easier. That's why I do what I do—share my experiences so others can learn from, and hopefully avoid, some of the mistakes I've made. I know I've learned a great deal from people sharing their experiences living off-grid, so it's truly a pay-it-forward type of community.

One last point I want to leave you with: Even though living off the grid sounds like a life of pure solitude away from people, in most cases this couldn't be further from the truth. We off-grid folks consider ourselves part of a unique and special community. And I must emphasize the word "community," as I have an entire list of people I can call and they would show up to help me in any way they could, while never expecting anything in return. That's how we are: Treat others as we would like to be treated.

If anything, I hope this book motivates you to live the life you want, no matter what form that may take. Well, as long as it isn't running in the streets naked in clown makeup, as that would probably lead to living a life you don't want, in a cell with a big sweaty guy named Tank. ☺

1

My Story: How My Mobile Lifestyle Began

In the next couple of chapters, I'll cover how I started on my journey of living off the grid. I've included this information in some of my previous books, so you can skip ahead to chapter three if you've already read it. If you're still on the fence, though, it might be a good review to light a fire under your butt to get going!

If this is the first book of mine you've read, I would highly recommend you read the next couple of chapters, as it's my story, and I believe there are some valuable life lessons I learned.

DEALING WITH TODAY'S LIFE GRIND

As most of you who follow me or have read my book *Going Off The Grid* know, my journey didn't start on a whim. I constructed the foundation of how I live over a decade ago. It started as a desire to live more remotely and simply; then it evolved into a complete lifestyle change.

First, I think it's important to understand that I grew up in a small town in the mountains of California, so living off the grid in the Pacific Northwest is not as drastic a stretch for me as one might think. I did not go into this adventure completely in the dark.

During my life, I've lived in many cities across the country. As I've gotten older, though, I've become disenchanted with and disengaged from that type of living. Urban living is not a bad lifestyle; it's just not for me anymore.

Having grown up poor, in a single-wide trailer with very few neighbors, you might think I'd never want to return to such a lifestyle. But that couldn't be further from the truth. Growing up that way has given me a unique perspective and shaped my thoughts about what's truly important. Sure, at times things were tough when I was young, but it made me appreciate everything I had that much more. I now look back and consider myself incredibly lucky to have had those experiences. I was fortunate enough to know most of the people in my town and was able to wave at them and get a wave back in return. That's pretty much unheard of in most urban settings today.

I still have fond memories of racing home from football practice before the sun went down to get in an hour of bird hunting. Heck, I would have my shotgun behind the seat of my truck to save time. Yes, that would mean I had a shotgun on school grounds, and I wouldn't have been the only one. A lot of us were hunters, and that was just all there was to it. Can you imagine what would happen to a kid doing that today?

Once I left for college at eighteen, I had very few opportunities to do the things I enjoyed doing while growing up—hiking, fishing, hunting, and just being in nature. And for many years I yearned to return to that type of living. It's hard to explain to someone who's never experienced this lifestyle, but spending time outdoors has always made me the happiest.

To me, the daily grind of living in congested areas has become completely overwhelming and stressful. Why would I want to sit in traffic if I don't have to? The thought of going to the mall actually makes me cringe, to say the least.

But I can't state this enough: There was a lot of planning required for me to transition to my current lifestyle, with numerous false starts and mistakes made along the way. With that being said, I wouldn't change a thing. Well, maybe I wish someone had already written the books I've put together, as it would have made my life much easier.

Like most people today, I was doing the day-to-day grind. I'd spent almost half my life working for the government in one form or another and was completely burned out and questioning numerous aspects of my life. I remember just sitting there at my desk, after another joyless meeting with one of my bosses, thinking, *What the heck am I doing with my life?* I knew I needed a plan, but what *was* that plan? I had a house that was ridiculously expensive, with more debt than I wanted or was really necessary, and I was living in congested southern California, slowly losing my mind.

I remember wondering back then, *Is there something wrong with me?* But since I've changed my lifestyle, I've spoken to and received emails from hundreds and hundreds of people who feel exactly as I did. I now know that the dissatisfaction I had with my previous lifestyle and mindset is not an unusual sentiment. If you feel this way, you're not alone. Today, there are a lot more people who are looking for, or who are actually living, the type of lifestyle I live now. Simply put, we're not willing to accept the modern-day societal expectation that we grind ourselves to oblivion chasing someone else's predefined idea of happiness... there has to be a better way!

The Search Begins...Kind Of

The original plan began simply with this: I wanted to find someplace quiet to get away to. So I started looking at remote land and cabins in Oregon, Washington, Wyoming, and Montana. At first, it was just a cursory look. As it was in the middle of the housing boom, I soon noticed that remote properties were just as overpriced as the typical single-family dwelling in more populated areas. I called a couple of realtors just to get some information, but nothing serious came of it. At this point, I was a little discouraged that my plan was nothing more than a dream.

So I shelved my plan and continued with my daily grind, feeling let down and not sure what to do next. What I've now found, after over a decade of research, is that everyone goes through this type of discouragement when they first start trying to make these changes. So don't lose hope.

Another important point I need to make is that I've never fit into the mold of today's typical American lifestyle: the nine-to-five job, the commute, the cookie-cutter suburban home. I started my own side business a good ten years prior to hatching my idea of a mobile lifestyle in an effort to break out, and I've always been more of a free thinker.

I knew that in order to really have freedom, I'd have to run not only my own life, but possibly my own business. Let me assure you, though, I don't think it's 100 percent necessary for you to run your own business to live a more mobile lifestyle—but it sure helps.

The best advice I can give is if you're feeling the grind, and really serious about living a simpler or more mobile life, you need to come up with a business model that fits in with your plans. Today, telecommuting is becoming more common for certain jobs that don't require you to be in an office day-to-day, so just because you have a nine-to-five job doesn't mean you can't live this type of lifestyle.

A Kick in the Butt—The Real Search Begins

Fast-forward to 2013, and all these thoughts were still in the back of my mind. But due to many life-changing circumstances, I wasn't really pursing my dream; I was in a rut. In that year, the stress of trying to run my own business weighed on me and numerous recent deaths of loved ones, including one of my best friends, hit home. I knew if I kept saying, *I'll get to it next year*, it would never happen.

So with that, I rekindled the dream and put a plan into action. From the time when I had originally thought about living a simpler, more remote lifestyle, my ideas had evolved and changed. I had started a new business, sold my house and most of my belongings, and was debt free. That put me in a much better place to really pursue my dream.

My original plan was to have a remote getaway; now it was to live off the grid for at least part of the year, dedicating myself to being more mobile rather than stuck in one place. I was fortunate, while working in the government, to have traveled all over the world, but that lifestyle was addictive. I had caught the nomadic bug and realized I could no longer just stay in one place for very long. In addition, the housing bubble had taught me that the supposed American dream of home ownership—with that big fat mortgage—is a chain around the ankle of a freedom-based lifestyle.

Most think that living a mobile lifestyle, or living off the grid, means living in a beat-up van, cave, or shack with no running water or electricity. Today, that couldn't be further from the truth. You can now live a comfortable life on a piece of fairly isolated land, or travel around in a state-of-the-art RV, and I know this for a fact! Not only have I been doing it for years, but I've run into more people than I can count who are doing the same thing or something very similar.

I'm going to address this now, as it's the main argument I get from people who think what I do is not obtainable for most people because I'm single with no kids. I could go into a long diatribe about life decisions and lifestyle choices, but I won't—maybe in another book (haha, just kidding.) The fact is, I've met so many people who are married with two to three kids, not to mention multiple pets, who are living *exactly* like I am. I'm telling you with firsthand knowledge, *anyone can live this lifestyle successfully if they want to.* It all boils down to whether you want it and will make it happen proactively, or whether you just want to make excuses and complain about your life. Yes, it's a little tough love, but someone has to say it. This lifestyle is as simple as coming up with a plan and putting it into action, instead of waiting for a miracle to happen, which will more than likely never occur.

I think the best part of this adventure is I'm funding it in a way that most Americans can afford. I don't come from a long list of millionaires, and I don't have unlimited resources. Still, I won't deny, it does cost money, especially in the beginning. I know there are shows and books that say you can just take off with a hundred bucks in your pocket and do it. And some people have done it that way, but I like to live in reality and talk about what's plausible for *most* people, not a select few.

I'm hoping you'll enjoy my adventure, and even if you're not interested in such a lifestyle, maybe you'll learn a little something that you can incorporate into your life to make it simpler and more enjoyable.

2

So Where Do You Start?
You Have Too Much Crap!

When you're thinking about living a more mobile lifestyle, or even contemplating simplifying your life, I think you need a solid starting point. As I preach in my other books, it's always better to have a plan and to take it slow in the beginning. Many people caught up in our society's instant-gratification thought process forget that great things come with time and perseverance.

My off-grid life and journey of simplification started several years ago when I decided to downsize. After owning several homes that were much bigger than I needed, and filled with crap I would never use, I decided it was time for a change.

The bottom line is, if you're truly interested in this type of lifestyle, you're going to have to downsize—and for most of you, you'll have to downsize big time! Don't be one of those people with a convoy of moving trucks moving all your crap from the city to the country. If you haven't figured out my philosophy of living off the grid yet, it's not just to relocate, but to live a simpler life. You can't do that with a ton of junk weighing you down.

CONSUMER NATION: BUYING EVERYTHING IN SIGHT DOESN'T EQUAL HAPPINESS

Just like most people today, I had spent my life being just what society and the system wanted me to be: the ultimate consumer. It's no secret that our lives suffer under maximum workloads in order to make money so that we can buy as much as we can to fill the unhappiness void. Now I'm not saying there's no value in work, and I don't begrudge working hard and earning an honest wage, but I do think we have our priorities way out of whack today.

Why do we purchase the biggest house we can obtain and shackle ourselves to its suffocating loan? Why do we buy that sports car we really can't afford? Why do we have a closet full of clothes and shoes we hardly wear? In the end, we stress ourselves out so we can obtain all these items, and for what? Exactly! You can't answer that question because there's no logical or reasonable answer.

To me the answer is simple: We do all of the above, and drive ourselves crazy in the process, because that's what we've been told to do in order to find happiness. So in today's society, stuff equals happiness. Trust me, I followed this mantra with gusto, purchasing all kinds of junk I didn't need.

Stop Being a Crap Collector

So where do you start? Well just like any addict, admit you have a problem. I like to attribute the moniker *junkaholic* to the affliction most of us suffer from today. As a human, it might seem like your primary goal in life is to compile as much useless stuff as you can, and then die among the heaps of your ingloriously obtained items in the hopes that someone finds you before one of your pets starts eating your face. OK, I know that's a little over the top, but I think you see my point.

Just as I said above, the starting point is realizing that your life means more than your stuff. You'd be more fulfilled by creating experiences rather than by acquiring shiny items. The luster of objects lasts for a very short time, then you need another shiny object to fill the void.

For me, I just had to realize that less was more. Just like my optimal health philosophy, the interpretation of *less* will be different for each individual: Having a more mobile life might mean keeping your house but having a getaway, or selling your house and renting, or going on occasional adventures in an RV, or going all-in living off the grid, or traveling in an RV full-time. As for me, I wanted to live in a comfortable, up-to-date home off the grid, but also spend part of the year going on adventures while towing a travel trailer. In other words, less junk, fewer headaches, and more time for what truly matters in life, while still living in the modern world part-time. I knew I wouldn't be able to do this if I held onto a bunch of useless crap, so I had to make a choice.

The starting point for me was to greatly downsize my living space. Back then, I was paying a ridiculous mortgage for a 1,700-square-foot house in southern California and losing sleep constantly trying to figure out how to pay for it. I was single and had two dogs. Why I thought I needed this much space, even today, is a mystery to me. Well, not really. I had been brainwashed into thinking bigger was better. In the end, all it did was stress me out, financially and emotionally, and make me spend a great deal of time on upkeep when I could have been using that time doing something I truly enjoyed.

There's one important point I want to make about our modern

maximum-consumption lifestyle: Instead of making us happy, it actually makes us less happy and takes time away from our true passions and the individuals we care about. If that isn't true irony, I don't know what is. We spend a great deal of our lives pursuing the things we've been told will make us happy, but in the end they make us miserable and unfulfilled. Wow, the joke's on us. The great news is that we can change this, and I want to share with you my experience and the steps you can take in order to *happify* (my made-up word) and simplify your life!

EVALUATE YOUR CURRENT LIVING CONDITIONS

The first thing you need to analyze is your current living situation. Can you get by with less living space? I would say almost everyone in this country could answer this with a resounding *yes*! If you live in a standard size American house and you say *no*, I'm pretty sure this off-grid or mobile lifestyle is not for you. But at the same time, that doesn't mean you can't take this information and downsize to a more affordable, smaller house. I know this book is primarily about mobile and off-grid living, but I'm a big believer in life simplification in general.

For those who are interested in life simplification, make sure to check out my **The Simple Life** *book series.*

The first thing I did was simple—I analyzed my monthly cost-of-living expenses. This included my mortgage, insurance, utilities, and general upkeep expenses and it came out to an astounding $3,500 a month.

For those of you who don't live in California, or one of the more expensive states, you're probably flabbergasted by that amount. Let me tell you, that's cheap in southern California. Most people

I know in California easily spend around $5,000 to $6,000, or more, for what I outlined above. Now that I look back with my "what's important to me" clarity, this was absolutely nuts.

I still had about 27 years left on my mortgage, so that meant I could look forward to spending a total of $1,134,000 (yes, that's over a million dollars) if I maintained that type of lifestyle for the remainder of my mortgage. But here's the kicker: Most of us don't maintain; we upgrade. So for many of us, that total would actually go up.

Basically, we all have the capability of being millionaires if we just adjust our lifestyle choices. That's a pretty astounding statement. Just thinking of the average person I know in California, their total would be close to double mine. I hope you're starting to see the insanity of our consumer-based economy in this country.

Most of you might think my example is rather dramatic, but I assure you, once I got settled in my new, downsized place, it was anything but. I was living in the typical southern California residential neighborhood in a home with three bedrooms, two bathrooms and a two-car garage. For a single guy, this is just way too much space. Heck, I think it's too big for the average family, but that's just my opinion.

Is Renting an Option?

The reason I bring up renting as an option is because it's a good transition if you're a homeowner who's planning to sell. Renting gives you a go-between while you downsize and get your plan together, but it avoids you having to make a big leap. It's getting your toes wet, wading into a simpler life in a smaller dwelling. Obviously, you don't want to rent a place the same size or bigger than what you have already; you have to downsize, which will force you to get rid of the dogs-playing-poker print on the wall in that dusty man cave.

That being said, I do know people who skipped this step, sold their house and all their stuff and never looked back. This all comes down to your goals and lifestyle plans.

After analyzing how much my house cost each month, I decided to take a look at renting and see what made sense. I realized I needed time to get my finances in order, work further on my business, and finalize my plan to simplify my life. The first place I checked out was Craigslist.com, and I'll tell you, it was very discouraging in the beginning; renting in California is fairly expensive when compared with the rest of the country. As I write this, another housing boom is overtaking California, and the prices are even higher than the previous one. I guess some of us never learn from the past.

Not to mention, back when I was looking to rent, it was just after the housing bubble had burst (the start of the Great Recession), so everyone was trying to do what I was doing. The glut of prospective renters was pushing rents even higher. The icing on the cake was having two large dogs; most rental owners really don't like pets, and if they do accept them they almost always hit you with a significant up-charge.

So what did that mean? Instead of renting in my general location, I had to cast a wider net in order to find more options. Having pets meant I had to look in more rural areas where people didn't care as much about renting to people who have pets. I began by looking for two-bedroom places and quickly realized the price difference between what I was currently paying and the prospective rental was not large enough to justify this choice.

This forced me to start looking outside my perceived comfort zone. I began investigating studios, granny flats (small apartments attached to houses), and cottages (basically a studio house in which all living space is concentrated in one area, as with a studio apartment).

This search led me to an entirely new lifestyle I had never experienced before and simplified my life far more than what I was used to. It's amazing: Having less space forces you to have less stuff, which ultimately makes you happier. I'll be honest, though, I really didn't see that happening in the beginning of my search.

Sometimes you might get lucky and find the place you want right away, but from my experience, making such a drastic change takes time. Here's why: Unless you've lived this way before, these could be neighborhoods or dwellings you've never experienced before and there will be some acclimation needed. You'll probably have to search in new areas you're unfamiliar with and determine which works best for your current situation.

And here's the key: Change is often painful in the beginning, and there's no getting around that. You have to realize you're making a major life change, and it might be uncomfortable at first. Most great things in life come with some scrapes and bruises along the way.

My search for a rental home in southern California took several months—six to be exact. I did a lot of research and soul-searching during this period, and, ultimately, it paid off. I found a cottage with a full-size yard located in a rural part of San Diego.

In the end, by being patient I ended up in the nicest place I had found and it had the lowest rent, to the tune of several hundred dollars! My landlords were also the best I've ever had. When you take your time and are patient, a little luck might come your way.

I will emphasize that when renting you need to really evaluate your landlords just like they're evaluating you. For most, moving is not a pleasant experience, so my philosophy is why do it more than you have to! When I moved into my new-to-me rental in San Diego, I knew I would be there for at least two years but I ended up living there for over four years.

That's another key thing thing to think about: How long do you plan to live in this place? Can you stay longer if need be? If you own, will you be able to sell your house in a timely manner, or will you have to try and turn your former home into a rental?

In my situation, I was unsure how long I would be there, but I made sure it was something I could do long-term if I needed to. Thankfully, I had thought that through, because I ended up being in the cottage rental far longer than I had originally expected.

I know most of you who are married and have children are thinking, *Yeah, that's no problem for a single guy, but our situation is different.* Yes and no. I know families who have reduced their living area by half with no problem at all. Sure, at first they and their kids had to get used to the new lifestyle, but once they adapted, I never heard one complaint about not having enough space. It's all about facing the challenge and not giving in to the sentiment that "it's just too hard."

Simplifying your life comes with challenges, and you have to keep your eye on the prize at the end. More financial stability and less stuff ultimately means more freedom. I'm not saying that minimizing your living space and having more disposable income is the solution to all your life problems. But I can promise you this: It's easier to figure them out without additional self-perpetuated stress.

The Payoff

The 2008 recession was not kind to most of us. I'll be honest, I ended up selling my house for a significant loss, but I had to make a critical choice: let the house eventually push me into bankruptcy or sacrifice short-term loss for long-term happiness. These were incredibly tough circumstances, but I don't regret what I did for a second. *I want to emphasize this is the decision I made, but I'm not a financial expert. You'll have to weigh your own circumstances and determine what's best for you and your family.*

The payoff for me was undeniable. By forcing myself way out of my comfort zone, I found a great rental home for a great price. Now I know you're wondering, *So how big was the cottage?* My new rental place was around 475 square feet (based on my measurements). That's right, I went from 1,700 to 475 square feet, almost a 75 percent reduction in living space!

Do I recommend everyone make such a drastic change? Of course not. Again, it depends on your situation and your comfort levels. I will tell you that I have no regrets and the thought of ever living in a big house again has not once crossed my mind since I made the change. I draw the above advice from my real-life experience. And as most of you know from my other books, I never give you advice about things I haven't done myself.

Now let's get down to the nitty-gritty—how much did I save? I was able to go from $3,500 in basic living expenses per month to $1,100 a month. The best part for me was not just saving a lot of money, but also not having all the stress of maintaining and paying for a large house. That was priceless.

Another bonus was that I had to sell a lot of stuff because there was no way it was going to fit into the rental cottage. I made close to $10,000 selling all my extra crap on Craigslist, and I sold most of it in 48 hours! I can't explain the cleansing effect this had on my psyche and life. After selling all those useless possessions, it felt as if a huge weight had been lifted off my shoulders.

I've learned that home ownership not only costs you financially, but it can also put you in a situation where you can get stuck. I used my time in the rental place to plot out my next move (which turned out to be my mobile lifestyle and off-grid project) and make sure I wasn't rushing into anything I would later regret. I know not everything can be planned for, nor does everything always work out perfectly, but I like to give myself the best odds possible to avoid as many pitfalls as I can.

Operation Travel Trailer: Hello, Tiny Living

As I explained above, this renting period taught me how to downsize; it also bought me time to get my ultimate plan together. By the time I'd been renting for about three years, I had purchased twenty acres of land for my off-grid house project. I was ready for the next step.

I found that while building a house off the grid, a great way to enjoy the property and save money is to live in an RV on the property. As a matter of fact, I've since learned that this is how most people build an off-grid house. For most, because there's no financing for off-grid homes, it usually takes three to five years to complete the project. The upside is you usually have no, or very little, debt when it's done; the downside is you need someplace to live for the duration. For me, I planned to live the mobile and off-grid lifestyle, so I now needed get a travel trailer.

For those interested in the off-grid lifestyle, I highly recommend you get my books **Going Off The Grid** *and* **Beginner's Guide To Living Off The Grid**, *as they're step-by-step how-to-books on planning and getting started with this lifestyle.*

Whoops, A Snag In Operation Travel Trailer

As I said in the beginning, I share it all, good and bad. I thought I had the perfect strategy living on my property in my travel trailer until I built my house. But this is where my inexperience with travel trailers bit me in the butt. At this time I had a 4x4 V6 Toyota Tacoma truck, and my travel trailer was an 18-foot ultra lite, which is made to be towed by smaller vehicles. There were a few problems with my plan, though:

- My property had terrible roads.

- The roads were very steep.

- My truck didn't have anywhere near the power to tow a trailer in those conditions.

- If I was able to get the travel trailer to the property, there was no way I was getting it out.

Luckily, I decided to do some recon before I towed my trailer up, and I realized my original plan wasn't going to work. Did I panic? Well, maybe a little, but what that did was make me look around for RV parks. I found there were more than enough in the area, and they ended up costing me only about $300 a month. I stayed at two different RV parks while building my house, and to be honest, it wasn't bad. In the end, it made running my business while building the house a lot easier than it could have been.

In the next chapter I'll share with you my story and adventures in RV land, and tell you why I think RVs are a great option for living off the grid temporarily, or even permanently. One of the most frequent questions I get asked, besides how did I find my remote land, is how did I figure out which RV to purchase. I also cover this material in my book *The Simple Life Guide To RV Living*.

3

Why RVs (Recreational Vehicles) Are a Great Option for Off-Grid Living

Before we dive into why I think an RV is a great option for a temporary, or even permanent, solution for living off the grid, I want to share my story of how I got started with my first RV. I'll also describe the various classes of RVs, because I get asked all the time what the differences are. This way, if you're interested in going the RV route, you'll have a basic understanding of the pros and cons of each class.

MASS CONFUSION, SO MANY OPTIONS

After purchasing twenty acres for my off-grid house, my search for other information started on the "dummynet." The internet is good and bad: Just as there's a lot of good information, there's also a lot of really bad information. Not only that, but when looking for product information it can be completely overwhelming. I recommend using the internet as a cursory search tool, but for you to do the majority of your research in person. Yes, that means investing in personal interaction with other human beings.

You can also join social media groups who are living the mobile lifestyle and search posts for the same questions you have. Trust me, you're not the only person who's gone this route, and you'll be able to ask questions of people who are actually living the lifestyle. I have to give a disclaimer, though, as some of you know my opinion of social media is not necessarily a positive one. You have to be careful in these groups, as they can be filled with people who don't know their ass from a hole in the ground, but love telling people their opinion. Again, don't rely on this method solely. You still need to get out and search for RVs and test out your plan yourself. Like I said earlier, this is *your* journey, so you need to figure out what's going to work best for *you*.

And I need to make an important point here. After spending several years living this lifestyle and talking to a lot of people, there's one common factor: In almost every case, a person's first RV won't be their last. As you get accustomed to the lifestyle and learn what options you need and want, you'll likely make a change. In fact, most of us make a couple of changes before we settle on the right RV. Plus, life situations change. You may have started out single and now you're married with kids, or it could be the complete opposite. With those life changes come different RV requirements.

I started by looking at various types of RVs, used and new, for sale on the internet. This didn't make me an expert by any means, but it did give me insight into the different types of RVs out there, and most importantly, what the heck one of these things costs. I'm not going to candycoat it—at first, I was completely overwhelmed by the options. Any simple search for RVs for sale will bring up hundreds to thousands of results, depending on your search parameters. Patience and due diligence are key. Take your time and don't rush into anything you'll regret later.

At that point in my life, I had never owned an RV so I was a complete rookie. My grandparents had owned an RV that I went on a couple of trips in, and I had several friends who owned them, but that was the extent of my knowledge and experience. Another important point: They were using their RVs for vacations. I was planning on *living* in mine for at least part of the year, so this was a very different approach.

Once I did my basic research, I contacted a couple of RV dealers and explained to the salespeople what my needs were, the extent of my budget, and how I planned to use the RV. Their answers would not address all of my questions, but they gave me a starting point to figure out what I was actually looking for and what the price range would be.

I knew it would be best to purchase a used RV for a couple of reasons. First, I had no clue what I was doing, so I figured the lower the investment, the lower the risk. Second, the price would be low enough that I could pay cash and not have to worry about carrying debt, just in case I changed my mind on this lifestyle down the road. There are many people who have bought expensive RVs, used them once, and now the monstrosities sit in their yards while the owners make payments for years for something they never use. Don't be that person!

Here's another option: I didn't do this, but for people who are really not sure about how far they want to go in this mobile or off-grid lifestyle, or even if it will work for them, renting an RV from time to time to test it out is not a bad idea. Here are some of the benefits of doing it this way:

1. The financial commitment is minimal.

2. You can test a variety of options before you purchase.

3. You can evaluate the mobile lifestyle and decide if it's for you.

In addition, if you're interested in living an off-grid lifestyle, renting an RV is a good way to get familiar with its many facets, including camping out in the woods or in remote areas.

Eventually I narrowed down what I was looking for: a travel trailer between eighteen and twenty feet in length, which is considered a small travel trailer by today's standards. The reason I decided to select this size was for two major reasons: First, I had a small truck, so I needed something small and light in order to be able to tow it. Second, a smaller RV meant a lower price of entry to get started.

I ended up purchasing a used eighteen-foot travel trailer from an RV dealer. The reason I ended up purchasing it from a dealer was that it came with a warranty. Unless you purchase a very new RV from a private seller, you get what you get. And I'll tell you, when something breaks in an RV it can be an expensive fix unless you're handy and know how to do it yourself. For me, it was worth a little extra money to have that peace of mind that if anything went wrong the dealer would fix it.

Here was my beginning setup: A 2005 4X4 V6 Toyota Tacoma, plus a 2003 eighteen-foot ultra lite (more on this later) tow-behind travel trailer. I bought both the truck and travel trailer used. The truck was $22,000, and the travel trailer was $9,000, so it was a total investment of $31,000. I didn't purchase them together, as I didn't have the funds for both at the same time, and bought the truck probably a year or so before the travel trailer.

I know some of you might be falling out of your chairs thinking that's expensive and completely beyond your financial means. As I said earlier, you do need to have some money to get started. Look at it this way, though—this was my transportation and home all in one! When you look at it from that perspective, it's dirt cheap! Also, I made sure this was within my financial means. I paid cash and had no residual payments. I'm a realist and understand this may not be within your financial grasp, but you *can* do it cheaper. I'm just giving you an example of how I did it.

I would say, though, from my experience, this amount is not out of the norm for what people would spend to outfit such a venture. Some people spend far, far more than this because they have the money to do so. When you factor in that the average sale price of an existing American home in 2018 is $247,000 and new construction with land is $400,000, I consider $31,000 for complete freedom a deal!

RV CLASSIFICATIONS: IF YOU DREAM IT, THEY MAKE IT

When it comes to the classification of RVs, this is where most people have the most confusion and the most questions. There are five major classifications of RVs:

1. Class A

2. Class B

3. Class C

4. Travel Trailer

5. Fifth Wheel

There are even more sub-classifications of the above, but to keep it simple, these are the five primary categories you'll run into during your search. I'm sure some of you are saying, *What about truck campers?* which are campers that fit into the bed of a truck. Can you live a mobile lifestyle with a truck camper? Sure, but I've never met someone doing it because it just isn't practical. For that reason, I've chosen to leave that category off the list. Truck campers are primarily used for camping, fishing, and hunting.

In the descriptions below, I'll include what I consider to be the most common size and cost for new RVs in the mobile lifestyle. I could go into the weeds outlining new, used, all the specific sizes, floor plans, etc., but it would just get confusing. For that detailed information, you have to dedicate yourself to some good old-fashioned footwork and research.

There's no perfect classification for any one person or lifestyle. The class of RV you choose will depend on several factors such as:

- Budget

- Location

- Lifestyle

- Size of family

- Amenities required

- Size of towing vehicle

- Self-driving RV versus towed RVs

And before I get started, I need to explain one thing: Most RVs today come with *sliders* or *pop-outs*. These are expandable units that actually slide out from the RV, and they're of great benefit because they can give you a lot of extra room when they're expanded. The downside is extra room means extra money; pop-outs don't come free. Nonetheless, I would highly recommend getting an RV with one or more sliders. I've owned RVs with and without sliders, and I'll never go back to one without them.

RV slider

Class A RV

Let's start with the big daddy, the Class A RV, sometimes referred to as a motor home. These are usually completely self-contained, meaning they have everything a normal house would have, including a power generator for electricity. These are usually thirty to forty feet long and cost between $100,000 and $500,000 new. Some can go for over a million! A perfect example is what you see people using at large sporting events when tailgating, or what famous music bands use when touring.

Class A RV

The Good:

- Extraordinarily well-outfitted

- Lots of storage

- Big floor plans, with sliders for additional room

- No towing necessary

- You get to pretend you're a rock star!

The Not So Good:

- Expensive

- Terrible gas mileage

- Big, sometimes *really* big

- Can cause high-pucker factor when driving

- Often the most expensive of all RVs to maintain

- Usually require a mechanic who specializes in Class A RVs

- Special class of driver's license required

- People may think you're a rock star and ask you for your autograph

Class B RV

These are what we called conversion vans when I was growing up. Think of a cargo van converted into an RV. Even though these bad boys are small today, they come with a big price tag, usually in the $75,000 to $125,000 realm. They're usually in the twenty-foot range in length.

Class B RV

The Good:

- Convenient

- No tow vehicle required

- Small and easy to store

- Decent gas mileage

- Easy to maintain

- Suitable for normal parking spaces

- No special driver's license required for operation

The Not So Good:

- Smallest of all RVs

- Usually don't come with pop-outs

- Most expensive when comparing size to price

- No rock star bedroom

- Cramped for two people

- Almost no storage

- You'll wish you had more space

Class C RV

Of all the RVs, this is the one most familiar to people, and this is what most people rent or use for that summer camping getaway or cross-country trip. I consider this the go-between of the Class A and B RVs. It's a little confusing because you would think this would be called the Class B, and the Class B would be called the Class C. Hey, I just report the facts; maybe someone in the federal government named them! The price range is pretty close to that of the Class Bs, but these will go from the mid-twenties to low-thirties in length, so they're definitely bigger than the Class B.

Class C RV

The Good:

- Bigger than Class B

- Better gas mileage than Class A

- Has some storage

- No special driver's license required

- Doesn't require a tow vehicle

- Not as expensive as Class A to service

The Not So Good:

- Usually not convenient for long-term living

- Doesn't usually fit in normal parking spaces

- Poor gas mileage

- Most unstable to drive, as compared to Class A and B

- At most, usually only one pop-out

Travel Trailers

Travel trailers are probably the most common RVs used by people living a mobile or off-grid lifestyle. People often confuse travel trailers and fifth-wheels, but even though they look similar, trust me, these are very different animals in the RV arena. Travel trailers are often described as *tow-behinds* in order to differentiate them from fifth-wheels, because you tow them behind your vehicle using your factory tow hitch receiver. I'll describe the fifth-wheel differences in the next section.

Travel trailers are the RV with which I'm most familiar. I've owned three of them, and I'm actually looking to trade up and purchase my fourth in the near future. For me, this was the most practical way to go as it fit my nomadic lifestyle the best. That being said, there are many ways to go in this lifestyle, so don't rule out the other options. Travel trailers usually range in the eighteen- to thirty-foot range and can cost from $15,000 to $90,000 new.

One More Option: Lightweight or Ultra-Lite Travel Trailers

There's one more sub-classification of travel trailer I'd like to bring up. I've owned two *lightweight* or *ultra-lite* travel trailers. Companies like to come up with different names, but if "light" or "lite" is in the name, it's almost always referring to the overall weight of the travel trailer. Just like the name indicates, these trailers are lighter than typical travel trailers. Lightweight trailers have become more popular recently, as they're primarily designed to be towed by V6 SUVs or light trucks.

The upside is they're smaller and lighter; but the downside is they can be pretty pricey and not necessarily designed for long-term living. I would categorize these as ideal RVs for families who are looking to go camping a couple of times per year, who don't want to invest more money in a larger truck, and who have limited space to store a trailer. These are great trailers for people who want to explore, but live in a more urban area. They're also great for people looking to test out the more mobile lifestyle, as they're easy to find and rent, and you don't need a special vehicle to tow them. They usually cost in the range of $12,000 to $25,000 new.

Lightweight travel trailer RV

The Good:

- A huge variety from which to choose

- Come in lighter weight versions that can be towed with a V6 vehicle

- Have most of the amenities of Class A trailers at a fraction of the cost

- Can be detached and left, thus freeing tow vehicle for daily use

- Low operating costs

- No engine, so if repairs are needed you're not stuck

- No special driver's license required

The Not So Good:

- Tricky to maneuver via towing

- Larger vehicles required to tow larger trailers

- Takes time to get used to, especially if you've never towed anything before.

- Take more time to set up and break down

- Need a separate generator to operate all electronics when no plug-in utilities available

Fifth-Wheels

OK, this is where it gets tricky for beginners—whether to get a travel trailer or a fifth-wheel. There are two primary differences when it comes to these RVs: size and how they're towed. As described above, travel trailers tow behind your vehicle, usually using the factory tow receiver. A fifth-wheel uses a special receiver that's mounted in the bed of a truck over the rear axle. So instead of hitching it behind the vehicle, you hitch it into the bed of the truck. Because fifth-wheel trailers are attached to the receiver in the bed of your truck, they're better balanced and tow more easily than travel trailers. In addition, the overall length of your fifth-wheeler and tow vehicle is reduced when compared to a tow-behind travel trailer.

People who live long-term in areas and have a family usually prefer fifth-wheels because of their size and amenities. They usually range from thirty to forty feet in length. They're also much taller than a standard travel trailer, so the headroom is similar to a house. The additional size raises their cost to the $50,000 to $100,000 range new.

Fifth-wheel RV

The Good:

- Not motorized so can detach tow vehicle for daily use

- Much more space than a standard travel trailer

- Amenities are closer to a standard house, like a Class A RV

- Built more for families or larger groups of people

- No engine, so not stranded if it breaks down

- No special driver's license required

The Not So Good:

- Usually much larger than a travel trailer, so harder to park and store

- More expensive to maintain than a travel trailer

- Requires a larger vehicle to tow—trucks only

- Special receiver required, so additional cost

- Receiver is in the back of the truck bed, restricting regular use of bed

- Usually costs more than a travel trailer

The previous sections are just to give you a general idea of the different types of RVs—this is by no means an all-encompassing description of each. There are so many factors that are directly related to your goals and lifestyle, it would be impossible for me to cover them all. In order to determine what will work for you, you'll have to look at them in person, and I would definitely recommend looking at each type of RV to become familiar with them so you can make an educated choice before you purchase.

Again, I go into much greater detail in my book *The Simple Life Guide To RV Living*.

WHY I THINK AN RV IS A GOOD TEMPORARY OR PERMANENT OFF-GRID LIVING SOLUTION

You might be thinking it took me a long time to get to this list, but I wanted to cover a little background and my experience with RVs. As I've said, I get a lot of questions on this topic. Below are the advantages of using an RV during your off-grid adventure:

- They've been around for over 100 years, so they're proven to be a great way to live a mobile or off-grid lifestyle.

- When compared to building a house, they're dirt cheap.

- There are hundreds of different types and floor plans, so there's an RV for every type of lifestyle.

- If you have an off-grid property with good roads, you can build a slab, install septic, drill a well, and have an alternative power source, so you can come and go as you please (I've seen this many times).

- It's an off-the-shelf solution that's ready to go. Once you purchase your land, you can literally be living on it the next day with an RV.

- Today's RVs have four-season packages that make them more efficient if you're living in extreme climates.

- If you build a house or change your mind, they're fairly easy to sell.

- You can rent one and test it out before you purchase.

This might seem like common sense to you, but I have to bring it up as some people may be coming into this type of lifestyle with zero experience. If you plan to live in an area prone to tornadoes or hurricanes, an RV may not be a great choice, as they're much lighter than a standard home and not built to withstand this type of environment. Also, if you'll experience heavy snowfall in the winter, you'll more than likely need to build a pitched roof cover over your RV. Numerous people in my area who live in RVs all year, or who have them on their property in the winter, have them under a roofed structure. Since RVs have fairly flat roofs, if you don't clear the snow off, and don't have it covered with a reinforced roof (think of a large heavy-duty carport), especially if the snow is wet and heavy, a very big problem could occur.

As some of you know, I actually split my time into living in an off-grid home half of the year, and living in my travel trailer down south in the winter. I guess I could be called a young version of a "snow bird." It comes down to loving both lifestyles, which is why I recommend an RV, especially in the beginning of living your off-grid adventure. If you want total freedom to not only live off the grid but to travel as well, you can't go wrong with an RV.

On the following page is a picture of my current RV and tow vehicle setup.

My current truck and RV

Finding and Dealing With Contractors Can Be Challenging

Those who've read my book *Going Off The Grid* know I go into great detail about finding a good contractor, and what to do when you get a bad one. I ruffled some feathers with the information I included in that chapter, because I was pretty frank about my experiences dealing with contractors over the last twenty years. I've owned several properties during my life, including investment properties, so I've been dealing with the shenanigans of shady contractors for a very long time. I won't re-hash all the information I included in *Going Off The Grid*, but I want to briefly cover what you can expect when dealing with a general contractor in today's building environment.

After I released *Going Off The Grid*, I received a few comments and emails from readers wondering why I was using contractors at all, as their perception was that it's not really what the off-grid lifestyle is about. First, those perceptions are incorrect, as I've spoken with and met numerous people living off the grid over the years, and only a few did the entire project themselves. And second, from what I remember the individuals who *were* able to forego contractors were contractors themselves, so they weren't a good sample to rely on when it comes to this topic. I don't know about you, but I don't have the equipment to drill a well 510 feet (that's the depth of my water well) or install large propane tanks weighing several hundred pounds, so at some point help is usually needed.

The bottom line is, most people trying to achieve their off-grid dream will need the help of a general or specialty contractor at some point in the process. Unfortunately, over the last five years as the economy has improved, the contractor world has not only gotten worse from my perspective, but more expensive.

It's well known in today's labor market that there's a huge shortage of manual laborers and tradesman. I'm not trying to scare you off, but I want to make sure you take your time and do your due diligence before you get involved with a contractor on your project. It's another reason why I'm such big fan, for those starting out, of gettting an RV to live in, as it gives you time to figure out what type of structure to build (if you want) and to find the right people for the job. As with almost anything in life, especially attempting to live off the grid, rushing will bite you in the butt in the end.

One thing that's been incredibly frustrating for me is that I've seen a dramatic rise in the cost of using contractors, but the quality of work is going down. To give you an idea, from a basic laborer to a specialty contractor such as an electrician, you're looking at $40 to $120 per hour on average. And most of the time I find myself going back and fixing the things they did wrong. Luckily for me, I have a decent amount of experience in construction so I can fix most of their mistakes, but it still get pretty steamed that I have to do it. But the average person won't be able to tell when a contractor is not doing a good job until it's too late, like when the toilet or roof leaks.

Also, most contractors today want nothing to do with a project in a remote area or off the grid unless it's going to pay them big money. I've had a tough time getting contractors to even show up because it's not easy to get to my property (four-wheel drive only). So what's the answer? If you need a contractor, make sure to read the chapter in my book *Going Off The Grid* and/or go the do-it-yourself route when you can.

DO IT YOURSELF (DIY) WHEN YOU CAN

I won't candycoat this one: If you plan to live off the grid or in a remote area, you're going to have to get your hands dirty. If you're not willing to do this, and to learn a lot of new skills, I really don't think this life is for you. I've not only acquired a couple thousand dollars' worth of new tools, but have an entire tool chest of new abilities. Sure, some of it was painful at the time, but I don't regret it for a second as I saved a ton of money, the work I did was better than if I hired someone, and I have a great sense of accomplishment.

I'm not going to go through each project and show you how to do them, as that's not what this book is about. Today there are a ton of videos and books on do-it-yourself projects. Heck, that's how I learned to do things over 20 years ago when I bought my first property. I remember I bought two Black and Decker how-two books on electrical and plumbing, and I still have those books and reference them from time to time. I literally had no clue what I was doing, but I learned as I went along. I soon realized that contractors were expensive, so I'd better learn how to do it myself or make a lot more money! The payoff was that I learned a lot and made $50,000 on my first property in less than two years, which I was able to sell in two days. That positive experience got me started in my side business in the area of buying, selling, and renting properties.

Here's a list of projects you can do on your own with little or no experience, and save a lot of money:

Painting. The tools for painting are basically some brushes, rollers, painter's tape, a ladder and, of course, paint. I've saved tens of thousands of dollars by painting the inside and outside of my properties. The best part is, if you screw it up or don't like it, you can just repaint it.

Plumbing. To install your own toilets, sinks and faucets, all you need is a crescent wrench and some patience—it's much easier than you think. Plumbers today can be expensive and most actually hate doing these types of jobs.

Electrical. You can do your own wiring in outlets, faceplates, ceiling fans, and lighting fixtures. Make sure you read up on this first, though, as electricity can be dangerous. Turn off all power and purchase an electrical current tester (this will tell you if you what you're working on has power to it) to ensure you're working under safe conditions.

Flooring. Install your own tile and/or wood flooring. Over the years I've been offered multiple jobs because of my tile work. It's not that difficult, but many installers rush it, making it look like crap.

Window Coverings. Install your own blinds, curtains or other window coverings. I've done this on almost every home I've owned.

If you do just those projects on your own, you could save up to $25,000, depending on the size of your home. That's right, I didn't misplace a comma. For more experienced people who build most of their home on their own, the savings are in the 50% to 70% range, when compared to having someone build it for them. With all the property projects I've had over the last 20 years, I've saved hundreds of thousands of dollars by doing things myself.

Here's a basic set of tools I would recommend for anyone who's looking into this lifestyle and wants to, at least partially, go the do-it-yourself route (you can nearly build a house with these alone):

- A cordless drill and driver

- A miter saw with a 10- to 12-inch blade

- A miter saw stand

- A table saw with 10-inch blade

- 16- and 18-gauge nail guns

- A framing nail gun (optional, if you plan to do some serious construction)

- A 25- to 50-foot air compressor with a kinkless air hose

I kid you not, the above tools are the ones I use about 80% of the time on my own projects.

During the projects pictured on the next page, I took it up a notch and actually built some of my own furniture and did all the finish carpentry, which probably saved me in the $10,000 range. Not only that, the finish carpentry I did is considered more on the custom home building side, so I also increased the value of my home.

Here are pictures of my office desk and a custom windowsill I built myself (cabinets were off-the-shelf; I built the top and stained it).

My DIY office desk

My DIY wood windowsills

The best advice I can give when it comes to accomplishing your off-grid dreams is to do as much of it yourself as you can. Then bring in a trusted contractor who's a jack-of-all-trades when needed. I have a contractor who comes for a day every week or two, to help me on the projects I can't do myself, or ones that take more than one person. In order to gain confidence in his skills, I gave him small projects in the beginning, then increased the complexity once he gained my trust.

Are Tiny Homes, Yurts and Other Temporary Dwellings Good Solutions?

Before I jump in, I don't want to 100-percent rule out the above for anyone, as the home that's best for you depends on your own personal situation. With that said, I've researched each type of off-grid and mobile home extensively and found that building a permanent dwelling or using an RV would be the most effective use of my time and money. I get asked all the time about these types of dwellings, so I wanted to briefly cover them below. For more detailed information on various different types of off-grid construction, and on how I built my house, make sure to check out my book *Going Off The Grid*.

YURTS—TO ME, JUST A VERY EXPENSIVE TENT

When I first started my off-grid dream, I had big googly eyes for living in a yurt until I could get my house built. Come on, a round house is just cool, right? Obviously, I knew nothing about yurts, but those glorious remote and off-grid living TV shows made them seem so easy to set up and live in. But what I've found is that's not necessarily true. Below are the reasons I found a yurt to not be a good temporary or permanent solution.

Yurt

- There are only two major manufactures in the U.S. that I've been able to find, so depending on where your off-grid property is, shipping could be expensive.

- Some counties consider them permanent dwellings, so you may have to submit and be approved for a builder's permit (yep, my county was one of them).

- If your county requires a building permit for erecting a yurt, you'll have to get another building permit for your house if you decide to build one down the road.

- For what they are, I consider them to be really expensive. I priced out a small one, and by the time I would have built a platform and made it livable, I was looking at somewhere in the $25,000 to $30,000 range.

- From reading about other people's experiences, they tend to have mold and moisture-retention issues.

- They're not very well insulated, so you'll cook in the summer and freeze in the winter.

- You still have to outfit the inside like a normal house if you want to live comfortably.

In the end, using a yurt temporarily until I built my house just didn't seem like a good solution. I'm sure I'll get emails from people telling me how great yurt living is, but I'm just sharing my own conclusion from considering my lifestyle requirements. Don't get me wrong, I still think they're pretty cool, just not in my situation for my property.

TINY HOMES—ARE THEY A PRACTICAL SOLUTION OR JUST A PASSING FAD?

So what's a tiny home? A tiny home is a house that's constructed on a rolling chassis (like a travel trailer), or a permanent home that's 500 square feet or less in size. I'll be mostly focusing on the tow-behind mobile version, as it's the most popular of the two at the moment, but I think it's important to discuss both because there's a ton of confusion about what a tiny home really is.

These smaller travel trailer-type tiny homes are really popular with the younger crowd at the moment, but to be honest I'm not a big fan of these for several reasons that I'll outline in this chapter. If you feel like a tiny home is the best choice for you, though, I don't mean to discourage you from this route.

Tiny House Construction

The base upon which mobile tiny homes are constructed—the aforementioned moveable chassis—is basically a steel frame with wheels, much like a utility trailer that you would tow behind your vehicle. People either purchase plans that show them how to build the structure on this rolling chassis and do it themselves, or they pay a company to build the house to their specifications.

Tiny homes are built primarily with standard wood framing/ stick construction, like the typical wood-framed house you might see built on a plot of land. Though with mobile tiny homes, the house is built on top of a moveable chassis. These types of tiny homes are usually less than eight and a half feet wide and vary in length from twelve to twenty-four feet. They're restricted to thirteen and a half feet in height in order to fit under highway overpasses when being moved.

Why You Shouldn't Jump on This Trend

The primary reason these tiny homes are popular is that they're

Tiny home on wheels

mobile like a travel trailer, but cheaper than a standard home. In my view, though, mobile tiny homes are usually a horrible solution for off-gridders, people who are mobile, and simplified living enthusiasts. Here's why:

- They're trendy, and trendy things are often scams.

- They're actually incredibly expensive, with prices that frequently range from $450 to $650 per square foot (pre-built). In comparison, an average travel trailer will be a third to half this cost.

- They have to be inspected and registered by your local motor vehicle division, meaning you must pay ongoing, yearly registration costs.

- A tiny home will typically have higher insurance premiums than an RV.

- They're very heavy, usually over 10,000 pounds. In comparison, my traditional travel trailer weighs a little over 4,000 pounds.

- They can be dangerous to move because they tend to be very top-heavy.

- They usually lack plumbing; if you want standard RV-style plumbing, it usually comes with an upcharge.

- They're usually made primarily of wood, and are thus a fire hazard when compared to RVs.

- When compared to a fifth-wheel, the fifth-wheel will be bigger, have a nicer interior, be much easier to tow, and cost less.

I'm honestly puzzled by the mobile tiny home movement as a real off-grid living solution; RVs have been around for decades, and today are incredibly comfortable, at a fraction of the cost of a tiny home.

I recently went to one of the more popular mobile tiny home manufacturer websites and priced out one that was around the same size as my current travel trailer. It came out to $70,550, and I've seen them go for $100,000 or more! In contrast, I purchased my most recent all-season travel trailer brand new for $25,000. Don't get me wrong, the tiny home trailer was made from nicer materials, but it had no more functionality than my travel trailer.

I can't wait until all the people who purchased mobile tiny homes decide they're done with the trend and try to sell them. I'm fairly certain they're going to lose a ton of money, and that's if anyone is even willing to purchase one of these overpriced sheds on wheels.

OK, I know you're probably thinking, *Wow, Gary. Talk about putting on the negative hat!* Well, if you're new to my books or my writings, you'll learn I that I don't candycoat anything. I find a pre-constructed tiny home to be a complete waste of money. Not to mention, it's probably going to require a contractor(s). (Please see my *Going Off The Grid* book for an entire chapter dedicated to dealing with general contractors.) I would highly recommend not dealing with a general contractor unless absolutely necessary, not only to save money but also to avoid the pain and stress often associated with it.

When a Mobile Tiny Home Is a Great Idea

Now on a positive note, if you're fairly handy and looking for a challenge, constructing your own tiny home is not a bad idea. You'll be able to do it on your own schedule, as well as budget, and build it exactly how you want. From the discussions I've had with people building their own mobile tiny homes, they usually take from two to six months to complete, and they cost in the $15,000 to $20,000 range. As you know from my off-grid adventures, I'm a big fan of the DIY lifestyle, and this could be a great opportunity if you're interested in really testing your skills.

The upside to a tiny home is if you *do* plan to build a permanent dwelling off the grid down the road, you'll already have a guest house, or even a rental unit for extra income, for people looking to test out living off the grid. Also, if you're new to construction or DIY projects, it's better to cut your teeth on something smaller and less complicated than a standard home first.

A QUICK AND CHEAP GO-BETWEEN SOLUTION— THE HOUSE SHED

For those of you who are really anxious to get started but don't have a lot of money or building skills, using a shed as your initial living solution might be a way to go. Before we dive in, though, I need to make two very important points:

- Some counties won't allow you to live in this type of structure.

- If you have a family with small children, you run the risk of having child protective services called on you for having inadequate living conditions. This could possibly result in you being charged with child endangerment.

I wouldn't recommend a shed as a long-term solution, but trust me, I've thought about it. I built a shed at one time, but after realizing the solar batteries in it would off-gas, I decided it was probably not a good decision for me to try to live in it full-time. I do know people who've used this as a cheap solution for off-grid living, though, or as a hunting cabin.

What makes a shed a potentially easy solution is that it's not only cheap, but a lot of counties won't require you to get a building permit for it if it's under 200 square feet. Also, if you're not a handy person, you can get it shipped in prefabricated pieces to put together yourself or have the company assemble it for you. If you decide to go the prefabricated route, though, you'll still need to have a cement slab or pre-built floor, to the specifications of the shed, ready to go.

On average, buying a prefabricated shed will cost you two to three times more than than if you build it yourself. I have a friend who went this route and outfitted it with insulation, running water and a toilet for under $5,000. He didn't have a lot of tools or resources, so he bought a prefabbed shed and had it delivered, then did the finish work himself.

If you build a shed and then decide to build a house, you'll already have a storage shed ready to go. Another benefit is that sheds are pretty easy to move—if not too big, they'll usually fit on a flatbed tow truck.

The downsides are they're not really good for extreme cold or hot weather, and if you decide to make your shed comfortable for living you'll be spending a lot of money you'll never get back, as there isn't a lot of demand for used, lived-in sheds.

Would I recommend this as a good solution for most? Probably not, but if you're single and looking for a little adventure, who am I to poo on your dream? ☺

6

The Right Vehicle for the Job: Truck Size, Hauling Weight Capacity and Torque

I can't emphasize enough that having the right vehicle for off-grid or mobile living is critical. I ended up going through two different trucks before I settled on the right one for my needs, so I hope what I share below saves you some time and money.

After looking at a lot of other people's setups for living in more rural areas, I came up with my ultimate tow and work vehicle for the job. My goal was to accommodate the combination of off-grid living and towing a travel trailer thousands of miles per year.

My final setup has come from years of living a remote and mobile lifestyle. It may not be the perfect setup for you, but I found it to be the best for me after spending over six months looking at every make and model of truck in the three-quarter to one-ton classification.

Tonnage ratings for trucks used to mean specific hauling capacities, but that's changed in recent years. Trucks are usually categorized as light-truck, one-half, three-quarter and one-ton when it comes to towing and hauling ratings. The important thing to remember is that a light truck is the lowest and one-ton is the highest when it comes to hauling and towing capacity. You'll have to look at the specifications of the truck you're interested in to see the true hauling and towing weight rating.

Also, all automobiles today come with what's called the *Gross Vehicle Weight Rating* (GVWR). Before you purchase your travel trailer or fifth-wheel, you'll need to make sure your vehicle towing capability is rated high enough to tow it. This rating (GVWR), along with your truck's towing capacity, is determined by many factors, including engine size, gear ratio, wheel and tire package, cab and bed configuration, transmission and axles.

Oh boy, are we having fun yet? I know this is getting a little confusing, but we probably should briefly discuss foot-pounds of torque while we're at it. One of the most important specifications to look at when searching for a vehicle to meet all your off-grid and hauling needs is the amount of torque it has. Torque is simply the power transferred from the engine and transmission to the wheels. This is an oversimplification, but it's the best description to use when discussing towing and hauling. (I'm sure some engineers and gearheads are cussing at my explanation, but if you want to get in the weeds, there's a ton of information on what torque means on the internet.) Basically, the more torque you have, the more power you'll have to tow. You can have a massive engine, but if you can't transfer that engine power (horsepower) into torque, it's a waste of money and gas.

Here's a more rudimentary explanation: Just because a vehicle is fast doesn't mean it has a lot of hauling or towing capacity. If that was the case, people would be towing trailers with sports cars.

What's a Dually Truck and Is It a Good Solution?

For those of us who grew up in the sticks, *dually* trucks were, and still are, pretty common. So what's a dually truck? It's basically a heavy-duty truck that has two wheels on each side of the rear axle.

Dually truck

Are they better for towing? Simply, yes they are. Here's why: They have heavier duty suspension, transmission, and rear-end and gear ratios than your typical heavy-duty truck. These trucks are designed purely for hauling and towing heavy loads. Do you need one of these in order to live the mobile lifestyle? No, these are primarily used by people who have larger-than-average fifth-wheel trailers, big flatbed trailers, livestock or horse trailers. And if you're contemplating homesteading, you might want to consider a dually.

The downsides to a dually are they're…well, big, which means they don't get good gas mileage, they're expensive, and they're not usually as good off-road as regular 4-wheel-drive heavy-duty trucks.

If you're one of those people who plan to live in a monster-sized fifth-wheel instead of building a house on a remote piece of land, or are using that fifth-wheel while building your off-grid house, I would recommend hiring someone with a dually or larger tow vehicle to put it in place on your property. I consider this a cheaper and much safer option than buying an expensive dually that you may not need, or towing the trailer yourself with an undersized vehicle.

Gas or Diesel Engine?

Until my latest truck upgrade, which has a diesel-powered engine, I'd only owned gas-powered trucks. But now that I've owned a diesel-powered truck, I'll never go back to a gas-powered engine. Here's why:

- It has more torque than a gas-powered truck, which makes for easier towing.

- It runs at lower RPMs, meaning less wear over its lifetime.

- It gets better gas mileage, especially when towing.

- It has fewer emissions than previous gas-powered versions.

- It tends to be more durable.

The downside is diesel trucks are more expensive, particularly when including maintenance. But even with the additional cost, I consider a diesel-powered truck to be far superior to a gas-powered truck when living the off-grid/mobile lifestyle. And I can say from experience, people living the mobile lifestyle who are towing and living in trailers are driving diesel-powered trucks at a much higher percentage than those driving gas-powered trucks.

Air Suspension

This is an option for those who are planning on towing heavy loads or getting a large fifth-wheel or travel trailer. Even though heavy-duty trucks come with heavy-duty suspension, with the increasing options and sizes of today's travel trailers, and the heavy loads of materials you might have to haul to your remote property, you may want to upgrade your rear suspension to what's called *air suspension* or *air bags*. I don't want to go into all the various suspension upgrades for trucks, as there are numerous options to explore, but I do want to focus on the primary rear suspension upgrade for towing heavy loads.

The most common air suspension system places an airbag, and corresponding brackets, over the rear axle or leaf spring of your truck. But note that air suspension systems do not increase your towing capacity; the many factors in your GVWR determine this. So if it doesn't increase the towing capacity of your vehicle, why would you install an air suspension system? Because it can reduce rear vehicle sag and permit a smoother and more stable vehicle ride while towing.

MY TOWING TRUCK RECOMMENDATION

You can save a lot of money by purchasing the right vehicle out of the gate. For those serious about this lifestyle, I recommend at least a three-quarter ton truck, but optimal is a one-ton diesel truck with at least 800 pound-foot of torque and four-wheel drive. (I've never been able to figure out why you would ever own a truck without four-wheel drive, but that's a topic for another time.)

During my long search, which included looking at both three-quarter and one-ton trucks, I finally decided on a new 2016 Dodge RAM 3500 heavy-duty one-ton turbo diesel. The upside is I can tow just about everything; the downside is these types of rated trucks aren't cheap, even used. New, they range from about $55,000 to $70,000, depending on the package and accessories you pick. But if you're a savvy shopper you can get a good deal. I wasn't planning on buying a new diesel truck and was actually looking for a used one, but that changed when I was able to get my above truck for $18,500 off the sticker price, and my final cost with tax and license came to a little less than $53,000. Don't get me wrong, there were some sweaty palms going on. That was the most I had paid for a vehicle, ever! But as I write this, I've had that truck for almost three years and have not regretted my decision for one second.

Some of you might be rolling your eyes and thinking this lifestyle is a fantasy when you look at the prices I'm throwing out. But remember, this is a journey and you don't have to spend that type of money to do it. Your choices will depend on your budget and how much you're comfortable spending. I spread this out over several years because I needed to figure out what my lifestyle would ultimately be, and most importantly, what I could afford.

I know people who've started out by buying dirt-cheap used trucks and trailers. That being said, though, I would recommend a beginning budget of at least $35,000 for both a towing vehicle and RV if you decide to use a travel trailer or fifth-wheel in your off-grid plans. For some, this might seem impossible, but remember the prices I outlined earlier for the average price of a pre-owned or new construction home today. The above price is pennies when compared to that.

With the off-grid lifestyle, I say this time and time again: nothing comes for free. You need two things to get into this: a plan and money. Most people love to live in dreamland and think they can just barter and sell some pelts to get by. But I'm going to tell you firsthand, money is still how our society operates and it will do so for the foreseeable future. If you can find someone who will take labor and other items in trade, by all means do it. But for most, this lifestyle will require you to save and come up with a viable plan in order to achieve your off-grid or mobile-living dreams.

For less than $100,000, you can have a top-notch tow vehicle and a brand new travel trailer, fifth-wheel, or Class A/B/C motor home. Yes, that's some serious cash, but that's a small fraction of the interest you'll pay owning the average American home with a thirty-year loan. Not to mention, most people who borrow money for college today can easily go over this amount. You just have to put everything into perspective when looking at this lifestyle. To me, the above total is very reasonable when it comes to living a truly free life, the way you want to live.

Obviously, you'll need to factor in the land and infrastructure costs for your off-grid property. But don't panic and think you can't afford it. Maybe you can't right now, but in chunks you surely can. Remember, how do you eat an elephant? One bite at a time!

7

The Good and Bad of Being Your Own Water, Power and Sanitation Company

Some of the below information is covered in greater detail in my *Going Off The Grid* book, but I feel I need to include it, as without it this section could get a little confusing. Also, I want to share more specifics of the lessons I've learned with my system, including some changes I've made to it.

Humans have been using sun, wind and water as sources of free, clean power for thousands of years. Think of sailboats, sundials and dams as long-used examples of how these earth-given resources have been—and in many cases still are—used. But throughout mankind's history, and still today, there are entrepreneurs, politicians and others who have figured out how to sell and regulate something that's actually free.

Here's a perfect example of just how powerful the sun is: Every day, it produces 35,000 times the amount of the total energy required by all who currently use electricity! Plus, it's 100% green and free.

There's no better way to become self-sufficient than to take advantage of these ancient and unlimited power sources. Sure, they may not be as efficient as our modern power grid, but they're a great way to take one more step away from the unwanted control imposed upon us by government regulations and the increasingly influential grip of privatized utility companies.

When it comes to living off the grid, the steepest learning curve is for creating, managing and running your own utility company. I know for me, even after reading several books I was still pretty clueless. After five years, I'm just starting to feel comfortable with my alternative energy and remote infrastructure knowledge and skills. This is one aspect of the lifestyle that's incredibly individualistic, as there are several factors and variables. Most of us cobble together a basic system, and then continually tinker with it as we figure out our requirements and/or add more creature comforts.

This is where I list all of my infrastructure/alternative energy components and products. Trust me, this will save you a lot of time and guesswork when you're first starting out.

WHY WATER IS WORTH MORE THAN GOLD TODAY

When it comes to getting started with remote living, most people think of beautiful views, peace, quiet and tranquility. But there's one major component they almost always overlook, and that's access to clean, reliable water. I grew up in the high desert of California, which has historically been entrenched in water rights battles, so I knew that access to water was critical before I even began my search for an off-grid property.

It seems the battles that ensue over getting access to water are getting more heated every day. Large parts of the United

States are suffering from severe drought, wildfires and extreme heat. But having access to water is incredibly important when it comes to off-grid living—in fact, I consider it priority number one. As many of you may have heard me say during interviews, *If you don't have access to water on your off-grid property, you just bought a really expensive camping site.*

To drive home how important having access to water was for me, the first thing I did after purchasing my property was drill my well. This was before I designed my house plans, did any roadwork beyond making sure the drilling rig could make it to my drilling site, or even built a storage shed. My thought process was very simple: Without water, I'd only be able to use my land for hunting and camping. You may be thinking, *If you didn't know water was there prior to purchasing the lot, aren't you going against what you just said above?* Yes and no. I did my research before I finalized my purchase by calling around to well drilling companies to see if other wells in the area were close by and what they were producing. Any well drilling company will do a survey prior to drilling other new wells in the area.

It's important to do your research on this subject before you purchase your land because when drilling a well, there's always the risk you won't find adequate water, or it could be tainted by having too much clay, sediment or natural toxins that are harmful to humans.

With that being said, I've only heard a few stories during my life of people having to drill in multiple sites because of tainted or dry wells (wells that produce no or inadequate amounts of water), but I wanted you to be aware of the risks.

WHAT'S A WATER WELL AND HOW DOES IT WORK?

A water well is simply a hole dug or drilled into the ground that provides usable water for a property or homestead. We'll be focusing on a drilled well by a professional company. Can this be a do-it-yourself project? Sure, but for most of us this just isn't realistic. Therefore, I'll focus on how to hire a professional company to provide your property with a reliable water source.

Requirements and Expectations for Well Drilling

So what do you need to get water from deep underground? First, a well-drilling company will bring a drilling rig, which is a large truck that will use a metal pipe to drill down into the ground until a water source is reached. These tend to be very heavy, large vehicles. They need to be even larger if the projected difficulty of finding underground water increases, so having roads with good access is vital for your well to be drilled.

Indeed, you should never underestimate the importance of road accessibility for jobs that require heavy equipment. Because my roads were very steep and had loose, fine dirt, the drilling rig had to be towed to the drilling site with a bulldozer. To avoid such problems, if your property is difficult to access make sure to do a full site check with the company you plan to use. If the drilling pros believe their truck will have difficulty on your roads, ask if using a bulldozer to tow the drilling rig is permitted. These drilling rigs are very expensive pieces of equipment, and some companies won't allow them to be towed to a drilling site because of possible damage. It's always better to know in advance!

A common drilled water well consists of a drilled hole, a casing to line the hole so it doesn't collapse (usually a sort of pipe about four inches in diameter that reaches down to the bedrock), an electric-powered pump (needed to pump water from within the well to the surface), and a well cap (which stops contaminates from entering the well). Expect to pay from $40 to $50 per foot of drilled well depth for all the previous listed components. This is a general guideline, and will obviously change depending on numerous factors, but I've found this to be a fairly consistent cost estimate for a professionally drilled well.

Well pipe and freeze-free spigot

The well hole is simply a hole drilled into the ground by a drill bit attached to sections of pipe. However, these are not the same kind of wells your great-grandparents may have used back on the farm. Have you ever seen an old-fashioned well with a bucket on a rope attached to a winch? An outdated well like this might be 20 or 30 feet deep and would reach water caught in deep layers of mud, so it wasn't always very sanitary or pleasant to drink from but was what was available in simpler times.

In contrast, a machine-dug modern well is very deep, sometimes reaching hundreds of feet below the surface (my well is 510 feet deep). This lets you reach water that has passed through the layers of dirt on the earth's surface and has filtered down to the hard bedrock beneath. This water is very clean and pure and is exquisite to drink. In fact, once you taste fresh well water you'll hardly be able to believe you drank city water for most of your life!

Note that the depth needed to find fresh water in bedrock depends on the geology of your area. In some places in the country, you'll need to dig 800 feet or more to hit water reliably; other places require only a couple hundred feet. Well-drilling professionals will typically be able to tell you how deep they usually need to dig in your area to hit bedrock, which is an important number for budgeting since you're charged per foot of drilling.

Also ask about success rate: If you live hundreds of feet above a plentiful underground aquifer, it will be easy to drill for water. However, some areas have water running in cracks in bedrock, which must be blindly targeted from above ground to hit water, and success is not guaranteed. In such cases, if water is not discovered the first time, you may have to pay to drill more than once to find an adequate well site on your property.

With a modern well, drilling goes as far down as is required until an adequate supply of water is reached, and supply is measured in gallons of water per minute (the amount of water measured when pumped from a given well). There's no absolute on what's considered an adequate amount of water by the above standard; this is completely dependent on your needs and expectations, such as how many people will be living in your house.

A workable well usually needs to produce a minimum of one gallon of water per minute, and most wells will produce between three to five gallons a minute. So how does my well stack up to this, you may ask? This might shock you a bit, but my well only produces about 1.5 gallons a minute, which is on the low side. But here's where it gets a little tricky: The static line of a well is usually determined by how much of your well pipe is filled with water 24 hours after it's first drilled. My static line was 250 feet from the bottom. So as you can see, even though my gallons per minute are somewhat low, my static line is fairly high, which gives me well above the amount of water I can use in a day.

What I've Learned

I've been using my well for about five years now and I've learned a lot, as using an off-grid well is different from using one tied to the public water system. Below are the biggest takeaways:

- By jumping on getting my well done first, I saved a good amount of money. The price keeps going up and up, and more people want wells because of water shortages (good old supply and demand at work).

- Having access to pure, clean water is a huge health benefit. Most public water is loaded with chemicals and pollutants that can cause health problems.

- I don't have to worry about water rationing or my water bill going up.

- I'm more conscious of my water use than I was while living in a residential grid-tied home.

- My well pump is an energy hog, so the more water I use the more drain it has on my off-grid power system.

AN INTRODUCTION TO ALTERNATIVE POWER SYSTEMS

When it comes to living off the grid, there are many challenges. Probably the most critical, after access to water, is the question of how to manufacture your own power (electricity) for your off-grid property.

As I mentioned earlier in this book, by definition *off the grid* means not being tied to any type of public utility. Of course, you could still use an alternative power source while tied to the grid, but that's not complete off-grid living.

My hope is that this section will answer a lot of questions for those of you thinking about living off the grid and will improve your understanding of what may be the best solution for your needs. I'll go into a little more detail in this section, as I get a great deal of questions about alternative energy basics.

I will say this: The most effective and reliable system is one that incorporates all three of the primary alternative power systems, since they tend to be complementary to each other in varying weather conditions (more on this later). The problem in most cases is that this won't be a practical solution for most people (for example, if you don't have access to a stream for a hydro power solution). Usually, two of the three systems can be utilized by most off-gridders, but it depends on your specific property type and location. (Again, this goes back to the importance of forming your goals and doing research *before* buying land!)

Please note that this section is not intended to be highly technical or provide you with template systems, but rather to inform you about the most common alternative power sources, how they work, and what I used for my setup. There are numerous books you can purchase with detailed information about setting up systems from A to Z.

WHY A POWER SHED IS A SMART MOVE

A power shed is exactly what it sounds like: a shed that will house all of your alternative energy components (such as an inverter). Here are the benefits of using a power shed:

- It can act as both a power shed and storage shed.

- Depending on its size, it usually doesn't require a building permit (though this will vary between states and counties).

- The power inverter is a bit noisy (buzzes while power is being inverted for use), and keeping it away from your house means you don't have to be bothered with the ambient noise.

- Lead-acid-type batteries off-gas hydrogen and oxygen when being charged or discharged. Due to this, by code (in many places), they require proper ventilation. So it's just easier and safer to keep them away from your primary living quarters.

- You can use the power shed as a template for your primary living structure.

- You can use it as a ready-made structure upon which to mount solar panels. (Caution: If this is your plan, make sure to build a roof that has southern exposure, can withstand the weight of the panels and racking, and is away from any shade-creating structures such as trees.)

For me, building a power shed was a great way to start out, and I highly recommend you do the same. As described above, it gave me a place to store tools and other items while I continued to work on the property. Trust me, if you leave tools—or anything of value—outside, someone will gladly come by and remove them for you. Just because you're remote doesn't mean no one knows you're there. In small communities, everyone knows what you're up to, especially thieves, so building a power shed is a great way to protect your belongings as well as your alternative energy equipment.

I also used it as a way to experiment with what type of siding, roofing and color palette I would choose for the house. It's a heck of a lot cheaper and easier to change things on a shed than on a house if you don't like them.

My power shed

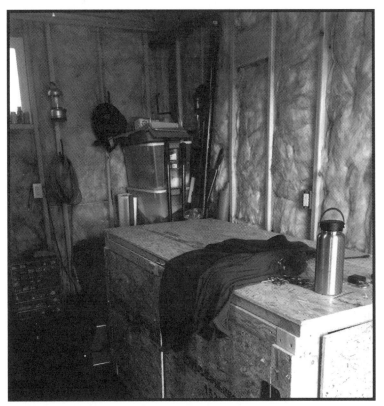

Inside my power shed

SOLAR POWER 101

So what is *solar power*? Solar power is when the sun's light or heat is converted into a usable energy source.

Solar power is becoming increasingly popular and more afford-able. Just like the technology behind computers, solar technology keeps improving, making it easier and more affordable to live an off-grid lifestyle with many of the amenities we've become used to in the modern world.

The two most common uses of solar energy are the genera-tion of heat and electricity. The use of solar for generating heat is usually in the form of *solar hot water,* those black pipes you see on house rooftops that help heat pool water.

The more common type of solar energy used today is the har-nessing of the sun's rays into usable electricity, typically via a solar photovoltaic (PV) system. These are the large black glass panels you see on rooftops or mounted on special frames on the ground.

Before we dive into a few technical points, let me just say that what I'll focus on here is true off-grid solar—that is, a stand-alone system that consists of the panel array, batteries, and a back-up generator that exists solely to provide power for you in your private home.

Now, for many, the first off-grid solar question will be, *Do we get enough sun at our home to take advantage of solar power?* Here's a great tool to estimate the amount of possible usable sunlight, wind or even geothermal in your area:

http://nrel.gov/gis/maps.html

And here's my simple way to figure out roughly how much available sun power you'll be able to generate per day using a solar panel system:

(Solar panels' combined maximum watt output) x (average hours of sunlight per day) x 0.5 = daily sun power generated

Note: In this equation, 0.5 is used as an estimate of power loss due to system inefficiencies and conversion factors.

Using my solar system as an example:

My system at this time consists of six 300-watt solar panels and four 315-watt solar panels, which gives me a possible maximum watt output per hour of 3,060 watts. To convert watts to kilowatts, divide watts by 1,000:

3,060 watts = 3.060 kilowatts

According to the map at the previous link, the average sunlight per day in my region is 4.5 hours.

So my equation will look like this:

3,060 (watts) x 4.5 (hours) x 0.5 = 6,885 watts of average power produced per day (or almost 7 kilowatts per day)

The above numbers, when compared to the actual power generated by my solar system, are almost dead on. But obviously, this will vary depending on the time of year, amount of cloud cover, and temperature.

How can you know what *your* daily power usage will be? The only way to determine this in an off-grid situation is to list every power-using item you have (or intend to have) and add them up. Now this method is not exact, but that's about all you can do for an off-grid situation. It's possible to design a solar array with the capacity to add extra panels at a later date.

Basic Solar System Components

A solar electric system is made up of much more than just a bunch of black panels. Here are the other components you'll need to purchase to make a complete system, as taken from the Backwoods Solar website. (By the way, I highly recommend you get a Backwoods Solar yearly catalog—it has a ton of off-grid alternative energy information and products. Backwoods Solar doesn't install off-grid power systems, but they sell all the components you'll need for your system. Better yet, they'll walk you through how to install them. I love Backwoods Solar and they've been an invaluable resource for me.)

Solar modules (panels) are installed in groups of 1 to 18+ modules on a solar mount, which in turn attaches to a building, to the roof of an RV, or atop a metal post or racks in the yard. Together this is called a solar array. Each solar module is wired to the other modules in that array by sunlight-tolerant solar interconnect wiring. Several arrays may be wired to a solar combiner box, where they're all connected to heavier underground wires taking the power to the battery and equipment room.

A *charge controller* is a small wall-mounted component which receives power from solar, wind, or micro-hydro generators, and controls the flow of power to the batteries. To prevent battery damage due to overcharging, the charge control automatically cuts back, stops, or diverts the charge when batteries become full. A charge control may have manual control switches and may have meters or lights to show the status of the charging process.

Batteries receive and store DC electrical energy, and can instantly supply large surges of stored electricity as needed to start or run heavy power appliances that the solar panels or hydroelectric generator alone could not power. This large power capability can be a fire hazard, just like utility company power, so fuses and circuit breakers on every circuit connected to a battery are essential. Battery size is chosen for both surge power requirements and for the amount of reserve power needed. Typically, 2 to 12 square feet of batteries weighing 150 to 5000 pounds are enclosed in a battery box with a vent pipe to the outside.

An *inverter* is the major electronic component of a power system. It converts DC power stored in batteries to 120-volt AC: standard household power. Short, heavy cables with a large fuse or circuit breaker carry battery power to the inverter. After conversion to AC, power from the inverter usually connects into the circuit breaker box of the house in place of utility lines. The house breaker box routes power to lights, appliances, and outlets of the house. The inverters Backwoods Solar offers for home power come in ratings from 300 to 8000 watts.

A system like mine, that uses components as described above, costs about $10,000 to $15,000, depending on the type and number of storage batteries.

Solar Power Limitations

Obviously, the biggest limitation you'll face with solar power will be how much sunlight you have in the area you plan to live. If you live in a place such as Arizona or southern California, there's a good chance you can get by just fine solely using solar power (with the right battery storage capacity).

But those of us in less sunny areas will need to have more than one alternative power system, combined with good battery storage. This is because when there's no sunlight (such as at night), you'll need to have the ability to utilize stored power from your solar or from the other components of your alternative power system. The same goes for less sunny days of the year.

A good battery bank is also important because the sun's light is not static, meaning you won't have full solar power utilization all the time. Instead, it will vary per the position of the sun throughout the day. (A note about batteries: These are currently the most finicky parts of an off-grid solar array, in terms of ongoing maintenance and replacement costs. I recommend carefully researching the pros and cons of different battery choices before making an off-grid solar decision.)

At the time I'm writing this, I have eight 6-volt lead-acid deep-cell batteries that are specially designed for off-grid power systems. One thing I didn't know before I installed my off-grid power system is that most storage batteries are not maintenance free. Like I noted above, they're a finicky beast and will take the most research and tinkering to figure them out.

Storage batteries

The model of battery I currently have costs about $400 and weighs about 120 pounds each. If you abuse your batteries, or don't follow proper maintenance guidelines, it will cost you a pretty penny! Probably the most important thing to remember, as far as longevity goes, is that no matter what type of battery you get, try to never discharge or let its charge go below 50%. On average I only discharge my batteries 25% or less, so I hope to get close to ten years out of my batteries before I have to replace them. But storage battery technology is getting better and better all the time, so I'm guessing when I do go to replace them I'll have much better and more cost-effective options.

Because the sun moves across the sky throughout the day, there are solar panel mounting systems that can either be rotated manually or that have small motors installed that rotate the panels gradually to obtain maximum sunlight. My first six panels are permanently mounted to my power shed, but I decided when I added my four additional panels that I would have them mounted on a pole that could rotate side to side and up and down to maximize the power of the sun throughout the day when my power requirements are larger. The sun will move up and down depending on the season, so you can also tweak the angle of your panels to get the most power possible.

I did look into the motorized systems that will automatically move throughout the day and track the sun, but I found they can be pretty finicky and were just not worth the money, as I can easily move mine by hand. I would highly recommend you have at least a portion of your solar panel array be movable for when you need to get additional power to run things such as a small air conditioner or your washer and dryer (which I have and am able to run at same time with my solar system).

The best advice I can give is that it's better to have too much power than not enough. Before I added the four moveable panels, I would have to run my generator far more than I wanted to, to keep my batteries charged or on heavy-use days or when it was cloudy. I can now run my portable air conditioner most of the day and still have my batteries 100% charged at sundown. I also did an experiment where I ran five loads of laundry in a row, starting in mid-afternoon, and again had close to a 100% charge in my batteries by end of day. Since adding those four additional panels I've yet to have to use my generator to charge my batteries, so I now know I have the right amount of solar power in for my system.

Moveable solar panels

Another effective solution is to install a complementary energy system to offset the limitations of sun power. For example, on a stormy, wet day, you won't get much sunlight and therefore not much solar electricity…but you may well have good wind or rain (hydro) options due to the turbulence and/or downpour.

WIND POWER 101

Generating *wind power* simply means using a wind turbine (propeller) to catch the wind and turn a turbine connected, via a shaft, to an alternator or generator in order to produce electric power. Essentially, the system converts mechanical energy (the movement of the wind) into electrical energy.

For wind power, I suggest using a small wind turbine (6-foot diameter or smaller) to supplement your off-grid alternative power system. Larger turbines can put out a great deal of power today, but the cost and size are not within reach of the average off-gridder. Not to mention, big wind turbines can make a lot of noise, ruining your remote, quiet oasis.

With that said, smaller wind turbines have become incredibly affordable: Many come in under $1,000 (not including installation). Once you jump past the 6-foot-turbine size, though, the price moves up very quickly. As an example, you can get a wind turbine in the 6-foot diameter range for $1,000 or less; a turbine with a 15-foot rotor can start to get in the $10,000 range.

On average, a small wind turbine needs about six to seven miles-per-hour of wind in order to produce a usable amount of energy. Depending on the speed and consistency of the wind in your area, a small wind turbine can produce enough power daily to run a small energy-efficient electric refrigerator.

The good news is most regions of the United States have sufficient wintertime winds to support most off-grid power needs. To find out how it's usually blowing in your area, use this winter wind guide:

http://primuswindpower.com/solarwind-solution/

Basic Wind Power System Components

The great thing about adding wind power to supplement your solar power system is that the components are almost the same. You simply tie your wind turbine into your solar power and battery storage system. The new wind turbines have smart technology, so they're already made to be tied into an existing solar panel system.

My System and Recommendations

As of this writing, my plan is to use a hybrid system of solar panels and wind power, but the primary source of my off-grid property's electricity is my solar system. This kind of hybrid system is the one I recommend, as it utilizes nature's two most accessible and reliable power generating sources. I'm at the top of a small mountain and I get more wind than other parts of the area I live in, so having a supplemental wind turbine makes sense for me.

Primus wind turbine

Here's a pretty important reason why I will, and you should, have two or more alternative power systems: At the time I'm writing this, the entire far west side of the United States is on fire. Even though none of the fires are close to my property, I've been engulfed by smoke for days as it blows from the areas burning as far away as California. It's affecting my solar system, as the smoky haze is blocking a great deal of sunlight from reaching my solar panels. During this time, the same wind that's blowing smoke into my area could be utilized as a source of power while my solar panels aren't working to their full potential.

My wind system will tie directly into my solar power conversion setup and consist of one Primus 46-inch wind turbine. And I'm contemplating putting in a second Primus 46-inch wind turbine, depending on my future power needs. This will bump me up to about five kilowatts of alternative energy production per day.

This may not seem like a lot of electricity production per day to most, especially when you consider that, according to the U.S. Energy Information Administration, the average American household uses about 30 kilowatts of power per day. But we off-gridders are not the average Americans, so in this case, the "average" number doesn't apply to most of us. Also, remember that my household at this time consists of just one person, so I'm able to use a smaller system than some. But I feel, with some conscious changes to energy consumption habits, most off-grid households could make my system work. In addition, off-grid homes will typically use a number of energy efficient appliances, and not some of the everyday energy hogs such as large air conditioners.

HYDRO POWER 101

For people contemplating living off the grid, or who want to supplement their current utility-tied electrical system, a *micro-hydro* setup is a great way to go, provided you have a stream running through your property. The downside: Regulations are changing all the time, so you'll have to make sure it's permissible in your city and county to use a micro-hydro system. Two things I can pretty much guarantee: It will require a permit, and it will have to be inspected and approved. There are two characteristics that determine how much power or energy can be obtained via hydropower: *flow* and *head*. Flow is the amount of water that flows past a given point in a given time period. Head is the water pressure, or how hard the water wants to flow. Higher pressure, water volume, or both will increase your system's ability to produce power. A micro-hydro system essentially consists of a length of pipe that captures flowing water in a downhill stream and then uses it to turn a turbine, thereby generating electricity.

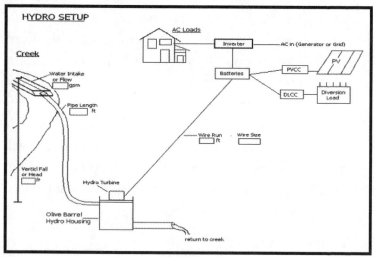

Micro-hydro setup

Per Backwoods Solar, you'll need to answer four questions to determine which micro-hydro system is right for you:

- What's the elevation change (from intake to the turbine) over the length of the pipe?

- How many gallons-per-minute of flow are there (minimum and maximum)?

- What's the size, type and length of pipe (if it's already installed)?

- What's the wire distance from the hydro plant (lower end of creek) to the home or power shed?

Just as with a wind turbine system, a hydro system can work off the same basic components as a solar array. Now you don't need to have a solar system to use a hydro or wind turbine system. Just note that the battery storage and DC-to-AC conversion work off the same components and principles for each system.

That being said, if you do have consistent water flowing through your property, micro-hydro is a great way to go. For that matter, many people use seasonally flowing creeks to supplement their off-grid system—your choice will depend on your resources and needs. Of the three main alternative energy-producing sources, hydro is considered the most reliable and cheapest because water usually runs 24/7, 365 days a year. Therefore, a hydro system is a continuous and cheap power source. This is why hydro is my number one recommendation for off-grid power.

When I was first looking at properties, I considered some properties with small streams running through them. I did this for two reasons: easy access to water and for generating power. In the end, I decided to purchase a property without a stream. Instead, I went for one with a great view.

This decision was made for several reasons: the prevalence of bugs that live nearby water in my area, the fact that streams can dry up at different times of the year, and the inconvenient truth that your power generating stream could be diverted away from your land by a property owner who lives higher upstream. I did initially try going for the off-grid trifecta: isolated land with great views and a hydro-worthy stream. However, this "perfect" situation was incredibly difficult to find, not to mention an expensive proposition where it did exist.

In the end, topography, shade, water access, the height of surrounding structures, your budget, local permitting and regulations, and your personal goals in going off-grid will all impact your decision of which type or combination of alternative energy systems is right for you.

GEOTHERMAL 101

Even though at this time I'm not planning to use geothermal power in any capacity as part of my own off-grid experience, I wanted to include it as an option in this text. That's because if you have the right type of property and can afford it, geothermal is a great option.

Geothermal is the only energy source that comes from the earth itself, and it's usually used for heating and cooling. Thankfully, this technology has come a long way, and it can now be used to generate power as well. Of all the alternative energy sources available, I find geothermal to be the most versatile and reliable. After all, the earth's core isn't going to cool down anytime soon! (And if it did, you'd have much, much bigger problems than which energy system to hook up to your new home. But I digress…)

The core of the earth is around 8,000 degrees Fahrenheit, so the deeper you go toward the earth's core, the hotter it gets.

Obviously, there's a great deal of potential free, constant energy directly under your feet. Geothermal energy originates from the inner mantle of the earth as hot magma (liquid rock) circulates upward while surface groundwater seeps downward. The magma then heats the water and forces it back up through faults and cracks in the earth's surface. When liquid forms, this geothermal energy is referred to as *hydrothermal*. The best part is that geothermal energy can be tapped into almost anywhere in the world! Though areas with volcanic activity offer the best geothermal possibilities, while highly elevated and mountainous regions offer the poorest.

The complexity and type of any prospective geothermal system will depend on how your area fits into the above rating system. There are many variations of geothermal energy systems, but I'll stick with the basics for now.

How a Geothermal System Works

As I stated earlier, the primary use for geothermal energy is the heating and cooling of industrial buildings and residential homes. However, with advances in technology it's now also possible to produce small amounts of electricity.

A geothermal setup sort of works like the solar pipe heating systems found on roofs that heat pools…only geothermal performs the same function underground. This is an oversimplification, but it's pretty close. In essence, with geothermal you're taking advantage of the consistent temperature of the earth, harnessing it through an underground piping system and then transporting it to the structure you wish to heat or cool. This piping system is called a *loop*, and it can be an open or closed system. The heart of a typical geothermal system is a ground-source heat pump that cycles water through the underground piping loop. *Closed-loop* systems circulate a water-based solution through a loop system of small-diameter, high-density polyethylene underground pipes, which can be installed horizontally, vertically or in a pond or river. *Open-loop* systems use existing well water or surface water.

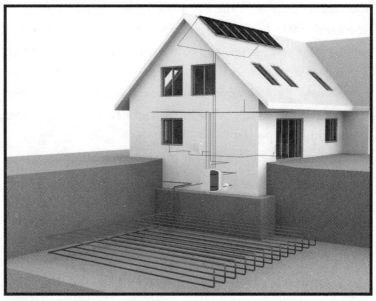

Example of home geothermal

During the winter, geothermal heating and cooling systems absorb heat stored in the ground via the water that circulates in the underground loop. This heat is carried to the ground source heat pumps where it's concentrated and then sent as warm air throughout your home.

During the summer, geothermal heating and cooling systems absorb heat from your home and transfer it to the underground loop, where it's then absorbed by the cooler earth. The geothermal heat pump uses the cool water returned from the ground to create cool, dehumidified air for your home.

For a geothermal system to make usable electricity, steam must be produced that spins a turbine attached to a generator that then produces electricity. This is how traditional geothermal plants have produced energy for communities for decades.

My Thoughts on Geothermal

As I've mentioned earlier, I have no plans to use geothermal on my property. When I was first starting out, I researched this option and received a rough price quote of $30,000 to $35,000 for a complete installed system, which is more than double what my solar and wind systems cost. My research also indicated that residential geothermal systems can produce electricity, but only in small amounts, so they're really not cost effective as you'll still need a different electricity-producing system of some kind. The biggest advantage of geothermal for people who live off the grid is that it makes it more achievable to have a modern central heating and cooling system. Another upside of geothermal is that, once it's installed, there are not a lot of additional costs. But because of the power that these systems typically use, they're usually not good options for off-grid living.

If you're resourceful, you can actually make your own geothermal system with ABS or PVC piping for next to nothing. There are plenty of forums on this topic that can be found via the internet, so if you have the time and patience this could be a way to go. The performance won't be as good as a professionally installed system, but from what I've seen, when done right they work fairly well.

The downside of a professionally installed system is, of course, the initial cost. Of all the alternative energy systems, I've found geothermal to be the most expensive. However, even though it's the priciest, it's also the most versatile and consistent of all the systems. Again, it all comes down to your budget and goals.

Why a Back-Up Generator Is a Must

Now that we have a basic idea and understanding of how we'll power our off-grid or remote property, it's important to make sure we have redundancies in case of a breakdown or unexpected event.

I can't emphasize this enough: Having at least one back-up generator is a must for people who are living, or planning on living, off the grid. Heck, I bought one before I even moved off the grid while living in the city, as a back-up in case of a natural disaster or when the power grid went down (and it did, big time, in California years back).

A back-up generator is simply a gas, natural gas, propane, diesel, or even solar-powered unit that can provide standard AC (alternate current, which almost all houses and appliances are powered by today) power when needed.

As a matter of fact, I haven't met one person who lives off-grid who doesn't have a back up generator of some sort. Most of us have two or more, which might sound like overkill, but let me explain.

As I mentioned above, I bought a back-up generator years ago when I was living in the city. If I remember correctly, I paid $500 to $600 for a Westinghouse 7500-watt gas-powered portable generator. This has been one of my best investments during my off-grid adventure, as I still have this generator and still use it to this day. The downside to this generator, even though it's portable (it has wheels and handles to move it around), is it weighs about 200 pounds when full of gas. Another downside is the bigger the generator, the more fuel it will burn. If I have to use this generator all day, which happened during some of the building process before I had power, it can cost $30 to $50 in fuel per day to run.

Remember, I also live in my travel trailer, which doesn't have a permanently installed generator in it. Don't get me wrong, I love the large generator I described above, but for practicality it's mainly good for one thing in an off-grid living situation and that's charging my batteries (I'll explain more on this a little later). My second, smaller back-up generator fills in the gaps that my bigger one doesn't:

- It's much lighter (though still a little heavy, around 90 to 100 pounds).

- It burns much less fuel, so it's better to run power tools when needed.

- It's much quieter; my big one is really loud.

- It has multiple uses and I can take it with me when traveling in my RV.

- If my big one dies, I have another one as a back-up.

When living off the grid, in order to charge your batteries in your alternative power system (such as when you have no sunlight for days), you need a decent sized generator that's at least 5000 watts or more; ideally, I would recommend 7000 watts or more. The main reason is that those batteries store a lot of power, so the bigger your generator, the more efficient it will be at charging them. I ran an experiment with my smaller generator to see how it would do on charging the batteries, and I'll tell you it was a total waste of time and resources as it barely moved the needle.

So what's my smaller generator like, you may ask? It's a Champion 3100-watt quiet gas-powered portable generator and I paid around $700 dollars for it on sale. The downside to these smaller generators is they can get really expensive—some are in the $2,000 range. The upside is the more expensive ones, such as the Honda quiet line of generators, are lighter, thus easier to transport. The most popular is the Honda 2000- to 2100-watt portable generator, but it's pricey (in the $1,000 range) and 2000 watts is not a lot of power. With one of these, you'll have to daisy-chain (connect two or more generators together) to get the power you'll need to live off-grid in most cases, or for your modern RV to run all your appliances. Below is a picture of my current two generators.

My backup generators

I hope you can now see the importance of having at least one back-up generator when living off the grid, but you may be wondering about the larger permanent-mounted back-up generators you sometimes see in Florida or East Coast homes that are exposed to severe hurricanes. I actually looked into that solution, but they're really expensive—$4,000 and up—and they can use a ton of fuel when operating. The upside is they automatically kick on when your power goes down or your batteries dip below the charge threshold you've set. But this type of unit only seems practical to me for homes that are in remote locations, and for people who have the money for them and really aren't into roughing it.

Yes, You Can Have Your Creature Comforts, But You'll Have to Make Some Sacrifices

When I first started on my adventure, I wasn't sure what kind of modern-day comforts I'd be able to have in my off-grid house. As time went by, I soon realized that alternative energy technology, especially solar power, has come a long way in recent years. Today, I would say if you want everything in your modern house off the grid, you can have it. But with that being said, know that the more power you use for these items, the bigger your alternative power system will need to be.

I will say, I've been pleasantly surprised at what I've been able to run with my small system. All I've had to add to my beginning system so far is four additional 315-watt panels, which at the time I write this are about $250 each—not too bad! On a normal sunny day, I produce quite a bit more power than I need, but it's nice to have it when I do need it. I'll even make this declaration: Anyone who walked into my home would not know it was off the grid if I didn't tell them. Yep, that's how far the technology has come. Here's a list of the items I have in my off-grid house that use power (some are propane-powered, but still require electricity to operate):

- A standard cooking stove with a vent fan above (the same one I had in my last grid-tied house)

- A standard refrigerator (smaller than your average one, but still big enough for a family of three to four people)

- A tankless water heater

- Two TVs

- A laser printer

- A computer

- A paper shredder

- LED lighting throughout

- Two ceiling fans

- A portable 12,000 BTU air conditioner

- A wall heater

- A stackable washer/dryer

- Basic appliances—toaster, blender, coffee grinder, etc.

As you can see, the items above are pretty much what today's average house contains. Now below are some of the things I sacrificed because I either didn't think they were necessary, or they consumed too much power for my system:

- Central heating and cooling (my house is very energy-efficient, but I can't power this type of system with my current alternative power setup)

- A dishwasher

- A microwave (I don't use them, but I could have one if I wanted)

That's it! Not much of a list, is it? And you can have these items if you want—you'll just have to add a bigger alternative energy power system.

The takeaway is that you can live with as many or as few modern creature comforts as you want. Obviously, it's a little more complicated off the grid, but it can be done.

10

The Importance of Fireproofing Your Off-Grid Home and Property

Growing up in the mountains and living in southern California for a large part of my life, I'm very conscious of the dangers of wildfires. At this very moment, California is suffering from its largest wildfire in the history of the state, and to me that's scary. As I've discussed earlier, with the worsening of weather unpredictability and continuous droughts, fire is a huge threat to people living remotely or off the grid.

FIREPROOFING YOUR STRUCTURE

When I first started dreaming about living off the grid, I had big ideas of building a rustic cabin. But as I started the building process, I realized that was probably not the best way to go. Don't get me wrong, cabins are still probably my favorite structure, but when it comes to the danger of wildfires, probably not one of the best options. There are two main reasons I would discourage people from building structures primarily built out of wood or combustible materials:

1. They're a big-time fire hazard, not only externally but also internally.

2. The odds of getting insurance on this type of house are greatly diminished when living remotely, and if you do get a policy it will probably be expensive.

I was able to get a comprehensive homeowner's insurance policy because my house is built to code (therefore approved by the county) and because it's considered a fireproof structure. As a matter of fact, my insurance premium is less than it was for the last home I owned in southern California, which I wasn't expecting.

As some of you might know, I used a type of green building brick called Faswall on my home, which is considered an *ICF* material (insulated concrete form). These are formed bricks made of 85% wood chips and 15% concrete, which contain rigid foam attached to the inside of the brick cell, facing the outside of the structure. In addition to having excellent insulation value, Faswall is also considered fire-resistant, and those are the two main reasons I picked this product. But just because *I* used this type of product doesn't mean it's cost effective or will fit *your* construction needs. I just wanted to share the product I used for those who are looking for a product that has high insulation value and is considered fire-resistant.

In addition to using a fire-resistant product for the main part of my structure, I also used other fireproof and fire-resistant products. Following are a couple of products I used to further make my house less likely to catch on fire or suffer fire damage.

Metal roof. This is pretty straightforward, as metal roofs don't catch on fire. The downside is they're more expensive, and transfer heat and cold more, than traditional shingled roofs.

Fiber cement siding, eves, soffits and fascia. Fiber cement has been around for over 100 years, and I absolutely love the product. It's durable, affordable, and can mimic the look of clapboard wood, shingles or even stone or brick. Basically, it's a building material made from wood pulp and portland cement that's weather- and fire-resistant. Most home destruction from wildfires starts with embers getting underneath the eves and soffits of your roof. You can eliminate this possibility by using the above product, which won't catch fire as a traditional wood product will. Below are some of the other benefits of fiber cement products:

- Long lasting

- Fire- and heat-resistant

- Weather-resistant

- Won't rot or warp

- Considered a green building material

- Fairly easy to install

- Expands and contracts less than wood

The great thing about using fiber cement siding, and other fiber cement building materials on the exterior of your house, is that even if you decide to use traditional wood framing, it helps a great deal to fireproof your structure. Also, it's very important to make sure you use the same process and fireproof materials for the surrounding parts of your home, such as sheds and garages.

As you can see from the picture below, my house and power shed are both built with the same fireproof materials.

Fire-resistant siding on my house

One last point I want to make is about how some of us love to go old-school and use tools from the past. I know a lot of people trying to be more self-reliant who like to use candles and oil lamps for lighting, but I would discourage you from doing this. One of the biggest dangers just a couple hundred years ago was house fires caused by the above. I think the current technology of LED lighting, which includes flashlights and lanterns, is a great way to go. Not to mention they put off much more light than a candle or oil-fueled lantern.

FIREPROOFING YOUR SURROUNDING PROPERTY.

One of the best ways to ensure your structure is safe from fire is to make sure you have taken the proper precaution of removing combustible items from the area surrounding your structures.

Here's a very important point I want to make: Make sure to clear your property of trees that could be a fire hazard prior to building. I've seen this time and time again: People clear a small area of trees around their building site instead of clearing the entire area. But once their structure is up, it's far more dangerous to remove these trees because they can fall directly on the structure. Luckily for me, my property was an old logging site, so a lot of the trees where I built my house were already removed. With that being said, I still removed several dead and rotting trees that were near my building site. Make sure to clear first, build second!

Here's a list of ways to make sure your property is less susceptible to catching on fire or having a fire that could engulf your home:

- Keep your stored firewood at least 50 yards from your home.

- Remove all dead trees yearly from your property, especially those close to dwellings.

- Keep all scrub brush trimmed down within 50 to 100 yards of your house.

- Make sure all additional storage dwellings are as fireproof as possible.

- Do not store gasoline or other combustible fuels inside or near your house.

- Have a pressurized water source near your home, such as a hose bib or no-freeze hydrant.

- Keep a fire extinguisher in all dwellings.

Obviously, there's no way to make your property 100% fireproof, but I think if you take the above steps, such as I have, you'll reduce your chances of having a catastrophic fire a great deal.

11

Why NO TRESPASSING Signs Don't Work Anymore

When I was growing up in the sticks, numerous neighbors owned several acres of land, and when you saw a NO TRESPASSING sign you knew that area was off limits. If you decided you were going to ignore it, one of two things, or both, would happen:

1. Your neighbor would come out to read you the riot act and tell you you'd better get off his or her property right now!

2. Your neighbor would call your parents and ask them if you had failed basic reading in school.

Either way, it was going to leave a lasting impression about not trespassing on other people's property. I even remember hearing stories, growing up, about certain property owners who may possibly fire warning shots over your head. I can't substantiate such rumors, but I know as a young kid I would stay far away from a property where those rumors were attached.

WHAT'S YOURS IS MINE

In today's society of the "I'm special for just existing" and "I deserve a trophy for showing up" mindset, respecting others' property has gone right out the window. Basically, it's the attitude of "what's yours is mine," which is short for "I don't own shit, but I like your stuff and feel I should have access to it for free." Now I don't want to discourage people, or paint a dark picture about owning your own land, but I'll give you a little information on what to expect when it comes to trespassers and how to solve that problem. I've talked to a lot of people over the years, and a lot of us discuss the same issues of people just walking right past NO TRESPASSING signs like they don't exist; and worse, they'll sometimes even walk right through an open gate with NO TRESPASSING signs attached.

Below I'll share a couple of stories of what I've dealt with over the last few years that has left me speechless at times when dealing with people who lack all respect for others' property.

But one thing I want to explain first, as I grew up in a pretty remote area, is that when you buy a piece of raw land that's been vacant for decades, with no clear markings or borders, more than likely people have been using that vacant land to hunt, drive ATVs, hike, etc. Until you actually put some fencing and signs up, they'll probably have no idea it's been purchased and the new owner doesn't want them trespassing. Also, where I grew up there were people who owned large pieces of land that lived in other states and never came to the property, so people just used it as if it was public land and the owners really didn't care.

The area where I purchased my current land had been used for decades for hunting, shooting, riding motorcycles and hiking, not only by locals but by people from the surrounding areas. Shortly after I purchased my property, many other people also bought the property surrounding me. In addition, some of the land is still owned by small logging companies. Obviously, most of the people who had used these hundreds of acres in the past are not going to be aware that people have purchased and are now living in areas they've been using for recreational activities. If you choose to buy land in a sparsely populated area, some people will know right away you're new to the area and where you purchased your property, but it will take some time for others to figure it out.

So, at first, I would recommend being gentle with people who may wander onto your property, as you don't want to be considered the new jerk in town. I even have people who know me and are friends ask me if they can mountain bike or run on some of my roads. Of course I always say yes, as it's the neighborly thing to do. I have zero issues with people who ask me ahead of time, or are just curious as to what I'm up to as they see a house being built in a place they've been visiting for years.

The problem that many of us have had to deal with, though, are the idiots who just decide they don't care who owns what, they're going to do whatever they want.

As those who've read my book *Going Off The Grid* know, I ran into a problem immediately when the first night the drilling rig came up to drill my water well I had items stolen from it. At this time I had no signs or fences up, but who would have thought some moron would steal things off a drilling rig? Lesson learned. Needless to say, I started putting up gates, fencing, and remote security cameras immediately.

Even after posting signs and putting up some fencing and cameras, I would see the motorcycle and ATV tracks of people cutting through my property. As you can imagine, I wasn't happy.

Not too long after that, I was in the initial process of building my house and I heard what sounded like an ATV at the top of my property. I walked up and found two teenagers sitting on their ATVs, smoking what looked like a dark green leafy substance. I knew from the tracks I had seen previously that these were probably the two knuckleheads who had been riding around on my property before. I firmly let them know I owned the property and really didn't appreciate them coming onto it, as they had ridden right by one of my NO TRESPASSING signs. I told them to tell their friends too, as next time I would be contacting the sheriff and wouldn't be so nice.

Problem solved, right?

Fast forward to the next year. I again hear ATVs while working on the outside of my house, this time on the lower part of my property. I ignore it at first, as there are roads down below me which are on a large property owned by a logging company. I know they don't like people trespassing either, but when owning several hundred acres of land, it's difficult to keep people off of it when you don't live there. The sound of their motors keeps getting closer and closer, though, and now I'm seeing a dust trail heading up toward my house. I watch this group of idiots ride right through four NO TRESPASSING signs and an open gate, and one of them does a big rooster right in front of my main gate. They're literally 60 yards from my house, so I get in my truck and drive down to see what they're thinking.

A little side note: I'm almost always armed when outside my house on my property, and this time was no exception. The time before I was armed as well. Now you might be thinking, *Wow, Gary's nuts*. No, because first, there are a lot of big animals that travel through my property, which include moose, mountain lions, and even wolves from time to time. Second, you're your own security and police force in the sticks, and there are crazy people everywhere. Trust me, I've spent many years in law enforcement. That's why my neighbors and friends always call before they come up; sneaking up on me unannounced is a bad idea.

To my surprise, two of the four young men were ones I had previously run off the year before. At this point I'm pretty pissed off, especially at the one who did the rooster, which tore up my road. I un-politely told them to get off my property immediately (using some of the words I may have used in the military and law enforcement for emphasis), as I explained they had ridden through numerous NO TRESPASSING signs and were now parked right in front of one of my security cameras and my main gate. The reaction I received was not what I expected—instead of apologizing and moving along, one of them starts talking back to me saying they never saw any NO TRESPASSING signs, which was pretty much impossible. I'm not sure what goes through people's heads today, as I'm shirtless, sweaty, coated with dirt, and have a firearm strapped to my side, and this brain surgeon of a human is getting mouthy with me. I pull out my phone and start taking pictures of their license plates, then go to video. They now know I mean business and decide to bolt.

You would think after such a confrontation this group of idiots would be long gone. Oh no, two of my neighbors had confrontations with them after me. The funny thing is, I know the grandfather of one of the young men—oops!

Just a couple of weeks later, I hear what sounds like a motor vehicle racing around on the lower part of my property. I think there's no way it's the same group from before. Nope, it's even worse! I get in my truck and drive down to find someone stuck in a truck on the side of my lower driveway road. He's another younger guy, with a small child that looks to be around five years old. He gets out of his truck and almost falls over—it's very apparent he's drunk off his ass. I tell him he's trespassing and needs to get off my property, as he drove through numerous NO TRESPASSING signs. In a loud voice he says, "You know me, man." I have no idea who this guy is (yes, I'm armed yet again and this is one of the reasons why), but he swears I know him. Then he gets in my face and asks me why I'm being such an asshole. Oh boy, now I'm seeing red.

I come to find out this dumbass is my new neighbor who I've never met, so he definitely knows whose property is whose and what roads lead to those properties. I tell him he has five minutes to get his truck unstuck and leave, as I know this is not a good situation and could lead to a possible dangerous confrontation. Fortunately, he finally leaves. It appears that he not only wore out his welcome with his neighbors, but his wife kicked him out shortly after, as I've never seen him again.

I don't want it to sound like you're going to be chasing people off your property every day, but some people think that just because they live remotely they won't have neighbors or people coming onto their property, which in most cases is the wrong assumption.

Meth Heads Are Everywhere

It's no secret today that America has a huge substance abuse problem. Methamphetamine and prescription opiate addiction are running rampant in rural parts of the country, so you'll more than likely run into a user/addict at some point while living remotely. The reason I bring this up is they're going to test you to see if you're a soft target to steal from and they'll completely ignore all your NO TRESPASSING signs on purpose to see if anyone will notice they're around. I've caught a couple of these individuals over the years roaming around my neighbors' and my property. They'll always give the excuse that they didn't see any NO TRESPASSING signs and they're just wandering around exploring. Don't fall for their crap story, though, and make sure you're very firm with them that they're on private property and they're not to return for any reason.

Just like the examples of my above disrespecting trespassers, the meth head has a problem with reading and seeing in the color spectrum of red.

How to Best Protect Your Property Against Trespassers and Thieves

There's no perfect way to keep unwanted people from coming onto your property, but below are some steps you can take to make it more difficult:

Put up several NO TRESPASSING signs. *But Gary, you just said they don't work.* Not always, but the law-abiding citizen will obey them. In addition, if you do have to report a repeat trespasser to local law enforcement, it's difficult to make your case if you don't have them clearly posted.

Have multiple gates. I have gates on all of the access roads to my property. I keep them all shut and locked, even when I'm home. Trust me, if you leave them open, some dummy will blow right through them as if they weren't there.

Use security cameras. I have several wireless cameras that send real-time information to my smartphone and laptop.

Get a dog. Dogs scare people who are up to no good, especially meth heads.

I have an entire chapter on security in my book *Going Off The Grid*, so if you want even more information on how to secure your property I highly recommend you purchase a copy.

12

Why Living Off The Grid Is Not Only for Entrepreneurs and Single People

This will be short and sweet, but there's one comment I receive all the time when it comes to living off the grid or living a nomadic lifestyle in an RV: "Gary I love what you're doing, but I have a family, so I can't do it."

Today, as Americans, it seems we have a built-in excuse for anything that takes a little effort or could be considered difficult. I don't care what your current living situation is: kids, no kids, pets, rich, poor—you get the point. Change is painful for everyone; you're not special. Every change I've made in my life for the better has had some type of pain factor associated with it. If you want it you can have it, but it depends on how much pain you're willing to endure. If you like easy buttons, I will say with 100 prcent confidence this life is not for you. You're going to have to learn an entire host of skills and become more self-reliant; period.

I've lost count of the emails I've received from people asking me questions such as:

"What type of RV should we buy?"

"What type of house construction should we use?"

"How many acres should we get?"

I very rarely choose not to respond to emails, but I don't respond to these types of questions because these individuals are looking for the easy button. Honestly, how can I answer these questions? These are pieces of your adventure and lifestyle *you* must determine; I can't do it for you.

Sorry, I got off-topic and on my soapbox for a moment, but it ties into the excuse of you can't do it because of "X" or "Y."

I've been living this way for several years now, and I'll tell you firsthand that single people and/or entrepreneurs are the exception and not the rule to this type of lifestyle. The majority of the people I meet living off the grid, or in an RV, have a family and a normal job. Again, if you have a family or a 9-to-5 job will it be easier or harder than someone who's single and/or who runs their own business? Nope, just different, as all of us have our own wants and challenges.

So the simple conclusion is: If you're married with kids, this lifestyle is achievable. And from what I see, far more people with families are doing it than single people.

13

It Still Takes Money

Another important point I must address is that many TV shows and blogs make this type of lifestyle seem like it's easily achieved on the cheap. Can you get a piece of land and construct an off-grid structure for a cut-rate price? Yes, but it's not the norm. If you want to increase your pain level, go out and attempt your off-grid dream with little or no money. I can pretty much guarantee it won't be a pleasant experience. Now I'm not saying you have to be independently wealthy either, but having a decent chunk of money with a set budget will make your life a lot easier, and your odds of success much higher.

There are two primary things you'll need to live this lifestyle:

1. A plan

2. Financial resources, including future ways of making an income

There's one common denominator for those who fizzle out in living off the grid and it has to do with the above two factors. I've seen it time and time again—most last less than a year without a plan and financial resources.

That's why I always recommend you pursue this type of lifestyle in phases. The first phase is to come up with a budget and save a bit more than you think you'll need. And if I can give you one piece of advice, it will cost more than you think it will—that's just how it works. You can't budget and plan for everything, as something will always occur that you didn't see coming.

The reason I harp so much on the financial part is that, at this time, you cannot finance an off-grid home. This may change in the future, but even then it won't be the norm, as banks consider off-grid properties to be a much bigger risk than traditional homes. The upside is when you're done with your house, you'll own it outright. The downside is you'll have to probably build it in phases, as you have the financial ability to do so. I know I spent five to six months working on my property, and then the remainder of the year saving for the next building season.

So if you're not good at managing or saving money, you'd better get your act together before you start your off-grid project. The last time I checked, the building supply store didn't take pelts or used furniture for payment!

With that being said, I would never discourage people from bartering for goods, as I do it myself. But you'll also need to have cold hard cash, as that's how the world works.

14

The Two Main Things That Are Stopping You From Living a Simpler Life

Simple living is easy. Well, easier than today's modern lifestyle, but getting there sometimes is not. I know, from the questions I usually get on the subject, that most people want to live a simpler and happier lifestyle but they're not sure where to start. I must emphasize this: Any time you make a fairly drastic change in your life, there's going to be pain in the beginning. Nothing that improves your life long-term comes easy—it takes work and perseverance.

I've found there are two main things that stop people dead in their tracks when pursuing what I like to call *the simple life*. I plan to expand on these two simple-living killers in a future book, but I want to share some of the basics here, to help you get started on your journey of happiness and freedom.

YOUR HEALTH

For those of you who've heard my numerous interviews over the years, this is not something new. I find it amazing that most people are dumbfounded when I say the most important place for you to start your journey to a better life is with your health. I can tell you, from decades of experience in the area of health and wellness, that this is something almost everyone battles on a daily basis. And I say this with great emphasis: Your health will affect you in everything you do in life, so that's why you must start here. How can you pursue your dreams and live simply if you're on three to five prescription medications (what most Americans are on today), are overweight (two out of three of Americans), are obese (one out of three Americans), are suffering from depression (one out of ten Americans, and rising), and can't live more than ten miles from a major hospital?

The simple answer is you can't! Here's the reason why almost no one starts here: because it's hard, really hard, to change your health.

You've spent decades destroying your health by eating nutritionally empty, sugar-loaded, processed foods, and not exercising, and you don't want to change. Almost everyone tries to shortcut changing their health for the better on the path to having more time and freedom in their life. As Americans we seem to think the easy road is the way to go. But I'm here to tell you that it isn't, and that you need to put on your big boy pants and suck it up. I know it's hard, that we've become sugar addicts, and studies have shown sugar impacts your brain chemistry similar to taking heroin or cocaine. No wonder your health is the hardest thing for you to gain control of.

Here's the upside, though: If there's one thing you're in total control of in your life, it's your health. You're the one who decides what you're going put in your mouth and how physically active you're going to be. Oh, I know, you're just too busy, you don't eat unhealthy like everyone else, and you'll get to it after you have more money and free time. I've heard all the excuses known to man, and they're just that—excuses!

Trust me on this: If you want more freedom, and to live the life you want, you need to get your health in order first. That's why I've included *The Guide To Optimal Health* in my *The Simple Life* book series. And in the future there will be at least one more health book in the series, because it's just that important!

YOUR FINANCES

Here's an alarming statistic: It's estimated that as much of 60% of the American population has less than $1,000 in their bank account and zero saved for retirement. Oh boy, we're in trouble! Just like your health, if your finances are in bad shape it's pretty much impossible to life a simple, happy life. Now I'm not talking about the famous line from the movie *Wall Street*, "greed is good." What I am saying is that money runs the world today and has for a very long time. There's no fighting it, it's a fact.

You don't have to be a millionaire to be happy, but it's sure easier than being dirt poor and constantly losing sleep trying to figure out how you're going to pay your bills. There's a famous saying: *Anyone who tells you money can't buy happiness never had any*. I don't know anyone who yearns to be poor, but, surprisingly, most Americans pursue being unhappy and destitute with unbridled passion.

We've been brainwashed to be the ultimate consumer and spend, spend, spend. I know, as I write this, that in order to feed this consumer beast, people want the minimum wage to be around $15.00 an hour. Now you're talking to a guy who made $3.35 in his first job as a young, bright-eyed teenager. The point I'm attempting to make is that most Americans make plenty of money. But just like our glorious fiscally broken federal government, it's not a revenue problem but a spending issue.

Let's apply some basic math to the proposed minimum wage. For example, let's say you and your wife are brand new to the labor market, you're making the proposed minimum wage of $15 an hour, and you work 40 hours a week.

Here's the equation for that: **40 hours x 2 (for husband and wife or two people living together) x $15 (hourly wage) x 14 (days for two-week pay period) x 26 (work periods in a year) = $62,400 a year.**

I grew up pretty poor, and this to me is a lot of money, especially when you consider this is proposed as a starting wage. This is not to disparage or argue for or against the proposed minimum wage, it's just to prove a point.

Today the average person will work for 40 to 45 years in America. Let's use the low end of 40 years, so that means, for a couple, the equation for life estimated gross earnings is $62,400 x 40 = $2,496,000!

That's right, even if you split that in half for one person, and if you never make more than $15 an hour, you still have the potential to be a millionaire in America! Let that sink in for a second. We don't have an income problem, we have a spending problem.

I have a book planned in the future on the topic of financial freedom, tentatively titled *Five Things That Are Making You Broke and How to Fix Them.*

With that being said, why does the average American have less than $1,000 in the bank or saved for retirement? Because we're not living within our financial means, which I can say with a fair amount of confidence is causing you to **NOT** reach your goal of living the life you want.

This is the advice I give to everyone who asks where to start with this lifestyle: Get your health and finances in order first, and then you can start to pursue your future life of freedom, happiness and simplicity!

My Top 10 Major Lessons Learned

Now that my off-grid and mobile-living lifestyle has been in full swing for several years, there are numerous lessons I've learned. Below, I list what I consider to be the top 10:

1. Having a plan and doing your research before you begin is critical.

2. Make sure you have financial resources before you start your off-grid lifestyle.

3. Unexpected events will occur; you have to be flexible.

4. The general contractor world is getting really expensive and the quality of work is the worst I've ever seen it. Learning at least some of these skills is important, both financially and for you to become more self-reliant.

5. If you can get an RV to your property to live in before you build your home, it will make the process easier.

6. Having a reliable four-wheel-drive vehicle is critical if you're going to be living in a fairly remote area.

7. There are bad people everywhere, and just because you live in the sticks that's not going to go away.

8. The off-grid community is incredibly helpful and just a great group of people to be around.

9. Even though you'll be living remotely, you need to have security measures in place, and I would recommend doing them before you build.

10. Know your neighbors—they could be a lifeline in case of a life-threatening injury.

I want to leave you with the main thing I've gained during my pursuit of living off the grid and a nomadic lifestyle: pure freedom! I don't regret pursuing this type of lifestyle for one second; my only regret is that I didn't start doing it sooner. Every night when my trusty Lab Barney and I go for our walk, smelling the forest, hearing the birds chirp, and seeing a running deer or elk makes me feel incredibly lucky.

It's not uncommon for me to lose track of the days, because I now live in the moment. I don't worry about the things I can't change, and I'm not rushing to work with tens of thousands of people stuck in traffic. As a matter of fact, there's no way I could return to that lifestyle. I've been offered jobs paying a good deal of money, but they all had one thing in common: living what's considered the American grind, and I just can't do it. This lifestyle isn't for everyone, but if you're looking to get out of the rat race and have some peace and quiet, I'm pretty sure living off the grid is for you. Heck, if you only do it for part of the year, or for vacations to get away, my attitude is why wouldn't you?

At the very least, I hope this book has given you some valuable information to make your decision easier, and to save you time and money if you do pursue your off-grid dream. That's what it's all about, after all: sharing my experiences and helping others.

For those of you who are truly serious about this type of lifestyle, I would highly recommend you purchase my book *The Beginner's Guide To Living Off The Grid*, as it's a companion book for this book and my *Going Off The Grid* book. *The Beginner's Guide To Living Off The Grid* is primarily a workbook to help you budget, plan and organize your projects. My main goal with these three books is to give you as many tools as possible to make your dream come true.

Did You Enjoy This Book? You Can Make a Big Difference and Spread the Word!

Reviews are the most powerful tool I have to bring attention to *The Simple Life*. I'm an independently published author and yes, I do a lot of this work myself. This helps me make sure the information I provide is straight from the heart and comes from my experiences without some publishing company dictating what sells. You, the readers, are my muscle and marketing machine.

You are a committed group and a loyal bunch of fans!

I truly love my fans and the passion they have for my writing and products. Simply put, your reviews help bring more fans to my books and attention to what I'm trying to teach.

If you liked this book, or any of my others for that matter, I would be very grateful if you would spend a couple of minutes and leave a review. Doesn't have to be long, just something conveying your thoughts.

Please visit Amazon.com to leave a review for my book(s).

Thank you!
Gary Collins

ABOUT GARY

Gary Collins, MS, has a very interesting and unique background that includes military intelligence. He's a former special agent for the U.S. State Department Diplomatic Security Service, the U.S. Department of Health and Human Services, and the U.S. Food and Drug Administration. Collins' background and expert knowledge bring a much needed perspective to today's areas of simple living, health, nutrition, entrepreneurship, self-help and self-reliance. He holds an AS degree in Exercise Science, a BS in Criminal Justice, and an MS in Forensic Science.

Gary was raised in the high desert at the basin of the Sierra Nevada mountain range in a rural part of California. He now lives off the grid part of the year in a remote area of NE Washington state, and spends the other part of year exploring in his travel trailer with his trusty black Lab Barney.

He considers himself lucky to have grown up in a very small town and has enjoyed experiencing fishing, hunting, and anything outdoors from a very young age. He has been involved in organized sports, nutrition, and fitness for almost four decades. He is also an active follower and teacher of what he calls "life simplification." He often says:

"Today we're bombarded by too much stress, not enough time for personal fulfillment, and a failure to take care of our health… there has to be a better way!"

In addition to being a bestselling author, Gary has taught at the university college level, consulted and trained college-level athletes, and been interviewed for his expertise on various subjects by *CBS Sports, Coast to Coast AM, The RT Network*, and *FOX News,* to name a few.

His website www.thesimplelifenow.com, and *The Simple Life* book series (his total lifestyle reboot), blow the lid off of conventional life and wellness expectations, and are considered essential for every person seeking a simpler and happier life.

Other Books by Gary Collins

Going Off The Grid: The How-To Book of
Simple Living and Happiness

The Simple Life Guide To RV Living: The Road to Freedom
and The Mobile Lifestyle Revolution

The Simple Life Guide To Optimal Health: How to
Get Healthy, Lose Weight, Reverse Disease and
Feel Better Than Ever

REFERENCES

"Air Suspension Basics for Towing." *Truck Trend*, 29 July 2016, http://trucktrend.com/how-to/chassis-suspension/1607-air-suspension-basics-for-towing/

Backwoods Solar, *40th Anniversary Edition Planning Guide & Catalog*. 2018

California Department of Motor Vehicles. *Recreational Trailer Endorsement*, http://dmv.ca.gov

http://census.gov/construction/nrs/pdf/uspricemon.pdf

DeGunther, Rik (2009-04-13). *Alternative Energy For Dummies* (Kindle Locations 3160-3162). Wiley. Kindle Edition.

http://gorving.com

http://legal-dictionary.thefreedictionary.com/Water+Rights

Morrison, Jim. "Commemorating 100 Years of the RV." *Smithsonian.com*, Smithsonian Institution, 24 Aug. 2010, http://smithsonianmag.com/history/commemorating-100-years-of-the-rv-56915006/

http://www.nrel.gov/gis/maps.html

http://primuswindpower.com/solarwind-solution/

http://ycharts.com/indicators/sales_price_of_existing_homes